ACES AND EIGHTS

Poker in the Old West

RALPH ESTES

TWODOT®

Guilford, Connecticut
Helena, Montana

A · TWODOT® · BOOK
An imprint of The Rowman & Littlefield Publishing Group, Inc.
4501 Forbes Blvd., Ste. 200
Lanham, MD 20706
www.rowman.com

Distributed by NATIONAL BOOK NETWORK

Chapter opener illustrations by davideser © Getty Images/DigitalVision Vectors

British Library Cataloguing in Publication Information available

Library of Congress Cataloging-in-Publication Data

Names: Estes, Ralph W., author.
Title: Aces and eights : poker in the Old West / Ralph Estes.
Description: Guilford, Connecticut : TwoDot, 2021. | Includes
  bibliographical references and index. | Summary: "Examines the role of
  poker in the lives of the fabled characters of the Wild West, and offers
  a portrait of the places where they lived and frequently died. This book
  offers both the 'facts' of these lives and the true tales of the game
  and the gamblers-and the entertaining 'tall tales' that have survived to
  this day"— Provided by publisher.
Identifiers: LCCN 2020038850 (print) | LCCN 2020038851 (ebook) | ISBN
  9781493049622 (paperback) | ISBN 9781493049639 (epub)
Subjects: LCSH: Poker—History. | West (U.S.)—Biography. | West
  (U.S.)—History.
Classification: LCC GV1250 .E77 2021 (print) | LCC GV1250 (ebook) | DDC
  795.4120978—dc23
LC record available at https://lccn.loc.gov/2020038850
LC ebook record available at https://lccn.loc.gov/2020038851

Contents

Preface

DEAD MAN'S HAND

"Take that, you lousy son of a bitch!"

Not the last words you want to hear, but they were all Wild Bill Hickok got.

As he pitched forward over the card table, his blood smeared the poker hand he was holding:

Two pairs. Aces and eights.

It was Deadwood, South Dakota. A town that's named for the lifeless trees in its gulch isn't likely to abound in glorious scenery. Any "glory" would have to come from the throng of saloons, dance halls, and gambling parlors. It wasn't even a legal town, since it was on Sioux reservation land that was supposed to be reserved for Indians.

Nuttall & Mann's No. 10 Saloon was less impressive than its name, a shabby log cabin with a canvas ceiling crudely covered with shake shingles. Spittoons sprinkled around in the sawdust. Dim lights, thick smoke, and wild, wild women—just like the country song says.

The long bar ran along the east side; it was topped with a scale for weighing the gold dust offered up by miners to pay for drinks and poker chips.

Wild Bill Hickok, famed marshal of the Old West, was not in Deadwood as a lawman or gunfighter. And despite what he told his new but absentee wife, he wasn't seeking his fortune in the mines. His target was the poker tables.

On the evening of August 1, 1876, one of the players at Hickok's table was a weaselly-looking loser named Jack McCall.

After McCall lost his stake, Hickok gave him a few dollars and suggested he get something to eat, but not to play poker until he learned how.

Now that would irritate a fellow.

The next evening Hickok was back in No. 10, clad as usual in frock coat, linen shirt, fringed leggings, beaded moccasins, waist sash, and of course his Smith & Wesson Model No. 2 Army Revolver. The seat normally preferred by Wild Bill, the one that backed up to the wall and afforded the best view of the room, was occupied by Charley Rich.

Hickok asked Charley to exchange seats. Rich just chuckled. "Don't worry, Bill, nobody's gonna shoot you in here."

Shortly after a grumbling Hickok sat down, Jack McCall entered, strolling along the bar until he was behind Wild Bill. With Hickok concentrating on his poker hand, McCall pulled his pistol and, with a loud curse, shot him in the back of the head.

Wild Bill lay dead on the floor, his blood-soaked cards splayed on the table. From that day forward a poker hand with two pairs, aces and eights, has been known as the "Dead Man's Hand."

And that's the way it was. Poker, in the Old West.

Introduction

"POKER MADE THE OLD WEST"

Not totally—but substantially.

If it hadn't been for poker, we might never have heard of Wild Bill Hickok. Nor Doc Holliday, Wyatt Earp, Calamity Jane, John Wesley Hardin, Lottie Deno, Bat Masterson, Belle Starr, and Luke Short.

These and numerous other "big names" in Old West history were gamblers first, gunfighters (and sometimes lawmen and brothel owners), second. Gambling was their livelihood; other pursuits just complemented the gambling. Their fame may have come from the barrel of a six-shooter, as the media of the day focused heavily on lurid stories of gunfights, not on accounts of complex poker games. As a class at the University of New Mexico described it, "penny dreadfuls, dime novels, and yellow journalism" were hallmarks of the Eastern media's coverage of the Old West.

For a full-time gambler, it was of course helpful to be good with a gun—or, more important, to be *seen* as good with a gun.

The competitive nature of poker did lead to frequent conflicts. When there was a table of players with big stakes, these conflicts could lead to violence. And when the players were armed, well . . .

Nowadays a professional or "house" dealer will quickly and authoritatively tamp down conflicts. Players who refuse to respond are likely to be promptly evicted. (In Las Vegas I've seen two burly bouncers heading outside with an offending player suspended between them, his feet never touching the floor.) Even in the Old West, a house dealer could call on the bartender or bouncers to reinforce his authority.

But a lot of poker was played in the Old West without an "official" dealer, just four or five players around a table—or a blanket on the ground. Poker was so portable, involving at a minimum nothing more than a deck of cards, that it could pop up anywhere: around the campfire on cattle drives, among soldiers in the barracks or on patrol, in stagecoaches on baggage spread across laps or the apron of a long duster, on riverboats, across hotel dinner tables, and of course on the hundreds of tables provided by saloons, gambling halls, and even whorehouses.

Adventure, land, greed, patriotism, curiosity, economics, escapism, ambition, opportunity—all of these contributed to the development of the West. But poker was the magnet that drew the gunfighters and sassy dames, the personalities that, fueled by the media, caught the public's eye and imagination.

The likes of Wyatt Earp, Doc Holliday, and many more were drawn to the scent of "fresh blood": those naive innocents who frequented the saloons, bordellos, and gambling rooms of mining towns, cowtowns, and railheads, and who represented easy money for the professional at the poker table. Earp, Holliday, and other cardsharps were good with firearms because they had to be, sometimes dealing with enormous piles of cash along with not-infrequent charges of cheating. Their shooting skills gave them a reputation that drew "young guns" looking to build their own reputations; hence, the shoot-outs and tales of bravado and derring-do.

Other than poker, there were plenty of ways to gamble, such as monte (often viewed as a form of poker), faro, roulette, blackjack, and dice. But those were purely games of chance; they involved little skill and a lot of luck. Only poker provided the opportunity to pit *your* skill and guts against those of another human.

So you could play faro, for example, everywhere, but (as long as it was an honest game) it simply involves betting on the odds of what card will be turned over next. There is no way for anyone to exploit their expertise over that of a silver miner, cowpuncher, or soldier. And without poker, one cowtown was no better than the next. But add a bunch of green cowboys just off the trail, and to an expert poker player, that town looks like El Dorado.

Without poker, the West would have developed, of course, but we wouldn't have had so many of the characters that gave it such color, notoriety, and even celebrity.

The Old West was synergism at work. The mining towns, railheads, and cowtowns were created in response to entrepreneurs, promoters, boosters, and expansionist corporations—not gamblers. New town, new workers, new population—plus fresh meat at the poker table—*that* attracted the gamblers, with their guns, knives, money, and chutzpah.

Inevitably there were fights, shoot-outs, and killings that drew reporters, authors, and photographers. The ensuing publicity fed outsiders' curiosity and drew them to those towns, causing growth to follow.

Eventually, as each town reached a degree of maturity, the new blood was no longer new, and the gamblers moved on to the next enticing opportunity. But they often left behind a bigger, richer, and conceivably better town—on its way to becoming a city.

Pure synergism.

In the longer run, poker not only aided in developing the West, it also impacted the culture, resulting in countless movies, songs, and of course books that drew on the players' notoriety. For better or worse, these various forms of media helped to establish the image we have of the Old West today.

Today poker is everywhere, especially on television, in shows like *World Series of Poker*, *World Poker Tour*, *High Stakes Poker*, *Poker After Dark*, and dozens more. Thousands regularly visit casinos spread all over the world, from Indian reservations to "riverboat" casinos that never leave the dock to the elegance of Las Vegas's Bellagio and Monaco's Monte Carlo (where the minimum stakes may be as high as $50,000). And then there's Internet poker, where you can lose your shirt before you get out of your pajamas.

So, is the poker you see today like poker in the Old West? No. Not by a long shot (although there *were* shots, of course).

I've played poker for over twenty-five years, in casinos, living rooms, garages, and bars. There were also some creepy dives (very bad judgment) where I was happy to escape with my life, disregarding the Franklins left behind.

Overall I've been a small winner, enough to salvage my pride if not to pay the rent.

But in the Old West, the *Wild* West, I would have been a babe in the woods, innocent of sophisticated cheating methods and unable to confront the six-gun or bowie knife in anything like a "manly" fashion.

This book is in no way a serious history of the West. What we think we know about the Old West is often challengeable, and a lot of it is flat wrong. The principals were prone to exaggeration, and even when they didn't purposely lie, they were often willing to let the wild fantasies slide by, as Bat Masterson did when asked about his supposed string of killings: "I haven't killed as many men as is popularly supposed but I have had a great many difficulties." (Bat's actual killing score was zero, or maybe one; there are conflicting stories.)

Legends can be a hard thing to stare down, so in this book I'm mostly taking them at face value.

CHAPTER ONE

Opening the West

As the Old West developed, poker became ubiquitous.

It actually started down South.

The first nonnative settlers in the West were Spanish. Corona-do's 1540 expedition, hungrily seeking the "Seven Cities of Gold" prevalent in Spanish mythology, got it going. By the early 1600s, the seven-hundred-mile El Camino Real de Tierra Adentro, "The Royal Road of the Interior Land," was charted, leading from Mexico City to the new Spanish territorial capital at Santa Fe.

Santa Fe was the center of trade up the Royal Road, and later down the Santa Fe Trail from Missouri as well. Its significance grew after it became a part of the United States in 1848. At the time writers usually described Santa Fe as just a collection of mud huts. In fact, those "mud" buildings were solid adobe, a material still widely in use throughout the dry Southwest. One of those mud buildings dates from the days of the pre-Columbian Anasazi and is considered to be the oldest house in the United States, located across a narrow street from the oldest church in Santa Fe (both can be visited).

The town of Santa Fe, though not large, contained a complex society that had evolved over two centuries from its first establishment in 1607 as the capital of Spain's northern territory: La Villa Real de la Santa Fe de San Francisco de Asís, or the Royal Town of the Holy Faith of Saint Francis of Assisi.

By the 1800s all this old stuff impressed neither the rough and rowdy traders nor the trappers and miners working the region. What interested them, beyond the profits to be made, were the gambling dens and fandangos—Mexican dances. After selling their goods and packing at least some of the gold and silver away for safekeeping, the traders spent their waking hours (mostly from dark to dawn) trekking from the card tables to the dances and back again, with occasional detours to a nearby bed.

Fandangos and gambling were constants—Sodom and Gomorrah in the mountains. Gambling was virtually a way of life among the Mexicans, as observed by Thomas James, who arrived in 1821 in time to participate in a Mexican carousal:

Tables for gambling surrounded the square, and continually occupied the attention of the crowds. I never saw any people so infatuated with the passion of gaming. Women of rank were seen betting at the tables. They frequently lost all their money; then followed the jewelry from their fingers, arms, and ears, then the rebozo or sash, edged with gold which they wear over their shoulders, was staked and lost, when the fair gamesters would go to their homes for money and redeem the last pledge and if possible continue to play. Men and women on all sides of me were equally absorbed in the fluctuating fortunes of these games. The demons of chance and avarice seemed to possess them all, to the loss of what little reason Nature had originally made theirs.

And the traders joined right in. The games could become wild and boisterous, and the vigorous betting, with bags of gold and silver, knew no limits. No limits indeed, especially when Texas and New Mexico were engaged.

Johnny Dougherty was a professional poker player, well-known around Santa Fe as very aggressive at the table. He and Texas cattleman Ike Jackson got into a no-limit game in Bowen's

Saloon. It was 1889, and they called it the Poker Championship of the West—sounds kind of like a precursor to today's World Series of Poker. A crowd of spectators jammed the saloon; everybody was there, including territorial governor Bradford Prince.

After a few uneventful hands, the betting heated up. With $100,000 in the pot, Jackson, now short of cash, scratched out a deed to his Texas ranch along with ten thousand head of cattle. He threw it on the table, stating that he was raising another hundred thousand.

Dougherty didn't have the money to call, but he did know Governor Prince. He wrote something on a piece of paper, drew his pistol, and handed the paper to the governor. "Now, Governor, you're my friend, but today my poker reputation is at stake, so you sign this or I'll shoot you." The governor just chuckled and signed the paper, and Dougherty tossed it into the pot, declaring, "With this deed I raise you the Territory of New Mexico." The Texan stared openmouthed for a minute, then sighed and laid his cards down. "You win, Johnny. But you're damned lucky the governor of *Texas* wasn't here today."

Roughly a hundred years after the Spanish capital of Santa Fe was established, the Spanish village of San Antonio was settled in Texas. Also about that time, New Orleans was laid out by a land company. The Big Easy was first French, then Spanish, then French—until it was bought by President Jefferson as part of the Louisiana Purchase.

The Spanish outposts of Santa Fe and San Antonio notwithstanding, in the early 1800s westward expansion ended at the Mississippi River. Its port, New Orleans, *was* the far West. Bright, loud, and bawdy, with streets lined with saloons and gambling dens and a multitude of hotels and fancy restaurants—and not a few low-down dives—it was a city without restraint.

There was little restraint in poker. It probably grew out of *poque*, a betting and bluffing game that had been introduced by early French settlers. Poque/poker readily took root in the freebooting atmosphere where wealthy farmers and plantation owners, soldiers, merchants, explorers, escaped convicts, and pirates roamed the French Quarter, some looking for fun, others—like the riverboat gamblers—for prey.

Entrepreneur John Davis provided New Orleans guests with the Davis Hotel, the Orleans Ballroom, and the Théâtre d'Orléans. "High-roller" gamblers were "comped" (the term now used in Las Vegas for "complimented," or complimentary) with free rooms, fine wine, and, of course, the best French cuisine.

The steamboat soon connected the Crescent City, as New Orleans came to be called, with commercial centers up and down the Mississippi, Missouri, Ohio, and lesser rivers. At the same time, traders were probing the West with mule trains and wagons, heading to Santa Fe and eventually California. Poker, which was wonderfully portable, always went along.

Up the river on the steamboat route, Natchez and St. Louis weren't far behind. But above all, if you were a gambler, *on* the river was where to find the action.

The larger steamboats on the Mississippi were smaller versions of the cruise liners of today. They went far beyond the merely utilitarian; many were floating luxury palaces. Crystal chandeliers and Persian carpets, hand-carved furniture and fittings, bone china, and the best champagne would be found in the elegant public rooms. Grand salons ran the length of the boat, replete with soaring gilded ceilings and mirror-lined walls (sometimes extending even to the engine rooms, perhaps to allow the engineers and coal-shovelers to preen before dinner?). The elite traveled first-class, their cabins fitted with luxurious beds, picture windows with constantly changing views, wash facilities, easy chairs, and even sofas.

For shallower western waters, builders devised "packet" boats, long, wide vessels of shallow draft and light construction. By the late 1830s at least twenty of these new steamboats could navigate in only twenty inches of water.

On the river, in steamboats large and small, tyros and pros intermingled. Sharpers were joined on the riverboats by wealthy farmers and plantation owners accompanying their cotton and corn to New Orleans, then returning up the river with sheaves of money. Whether "mainline" or packet, every steamboat shared one feature: poker tables. These not only afforded a comfortable way to pass the time; they also attracted the professional gamblers, whose classy, even "blingy," appearance helped "dress the boat," sending the message that a boat's passengers were of the better class.

Unlike the hoodies and reversed baseball caps prominent in today's televised poker tournaments, the attire of the steamboat gamblers was top of the line. The long black coat, satiny vest, ruffled white shirt, large knotted tie featuring a diamond stickpin— the bigger the better—all had a purpose: to clearly identify this person as both a *professional gambler* and a *person of substance*. Diamonds and gold were everywhere, not only in stickpins, but also in cufflinks and watches, diamond-studded golden pencils, and even gold-headed walking canes. Often a heavy golden chain would adorn the professional's neck—gambling dude Jimmy Fitzgerald's was nearly twenty feet long. These accoutrements were not only meant to impress; they could also readily be converted into cash if needed during a game.

Professional gamblers were, and intended to be, seducements for the backwoods grangers, western cattlemen, and aspiring California gold-seekers. Who wants to gamble with some rum-bum when you can challenge the top dog? Just as a famous gunfighter would attract the young punk who wanted to make a name for himself, so the professional gamblers were powerful magnets drawing the amateurs and tyros (that is, the suckers) to their tables.

But professional gamblers, even if they were expert cheaters, would sometimes run into a surprise—as we see in an oft-told and *possibly true* tale.

On a boat steaming down the Mississippi, an innocent young man joined a poker game of five-card draw. He and his new bride were returning from New York, where he had collected $50,000 from Eastern merchants on behalf of Southern planters. Unfortunately, the more he played, the more he lost. Ultimately the money was all gone.

In a daze, he slowly rose from the table overcome with guilt and ashamed to admit the loss to his bride. When he found himself at the boat's railing, he started to climb to what would be his death.

"Where you going, son?" A tall man laid his hand on the lad's shoulder, then firmly pulled him back aboard. "I don't think there's much down there to see."

The young man protested that, because he had shamed his wife and family, he wasn't fit to live.

The stranger teased him that things couldn't really be that bad, could they?

But no, the lad explained that Louisiana planters had sent him to obtain $50,000 from New York bankers, and he had lost it all in a game of poker—every penny.

"Lost it all in a game of poker, huh? Are you that bad of a player?"

"Well, sir, I have generally done well enough playing poker, but in this game I guess luck was just against me, for every time I'd get a good hand and bet it strong another fellow would have a better hand. Every time, it seemed. I couldn't believe it, which I guess is why I kept on playing. But my luck didn't change."

The tall chap nodded his head thoughtfully, saying that in his home state of Kentucky it wasn't considered a bad thing to play poker, and in Texas, where he was heading, it was virtually the national pastime. He then led the lad back to his cabin and ushered him inside to his wife.

After a few cordial words, the Kentuckian strode back to the poker table, inquired as to whether the empty chair was taken, and was welcomed to the game.

He began winning quickly, delighting the gamblers as he kept raising the stakes. They figured they would hold out some good cards, appear to just go along, arrange for the stranger to get a strong hand, and then pounce.

Soon the Kentuckian hit a particularly strong hand; the raises caromed around the table until an enormous pot was built. At the showdown a white-goateed Southerner, who at least *appeared* to be a gentleman, smirkingly declared, "Ah'm so sorry, suh, but Ah believe mah aces have you beat."

But the newcomer's hands were quick, and one now held a wide and very long knife. With his other hand around the gambler's wrist, the Kentuckian drawled, "Show your hand, sir, and if it has more than five cards I shall carve out your heart and add it to the pot." With that he gave a twist, and a sixth card fell from the gambler's sleeve.

"Well, well. I guess I'll just have to take this here pot. And you sidewinders would be wise to shuffle off this boat at its next docking. You won't be welcomed by any more poker players on this run."

Then the Kentuckian rose and ambled to the newlyweds' cabin. When they opened the door, he gently laid $50,000 on the table. As he turned to leave, the young man grabbed his sleeve, crying, "Wait a minute. Who the devil are you?" The soon-to-be-Texan's lips twitched into a hint of a smile. "My name is James Bowie, son, but I'd be pleased if you folks just called me Jim."

Competition among riverboats for luxury, style, image, and reputation soon became fierce. Naturally, this produced head-to-head races. Naturally, too, *that* led to a surge of betting. And when the race was over, winners and losers, with gambling fever still coursing through their veins, headed for the card tables.

Southern gentlemen, in particular, welcomed the card tables. As a man of the South you were expected to excel—or at least pretend to—whether with a gun or a deck of cards. And if you lost? You took it with grace and never a hint of regret, even when you had just gambled away the cotton crop proceeds.

Author Margaret Mitchell obviously recognized the gambling proclivity of Southern gentlemen. In *Gone with the Wind*, she has Rhett Butler describe himself as having "no training whatsoever to be anything but a Charleston gentleman, a good pistol shot and an excellent poker player."

Doc Holliday's biographer said Doc understood the propensity of Southerners to gamble because he was a Southern aristocrat himself. He knew that wealthy Southerners used high-stakes wagers as a way to display their competitiveness, their courage, and their materialism. Great gains as well as great losses served as symbolic testament to the cavalier postbellum lifestyle of the Southern gentry.

Justice on the river was usually meted out by steamboat captains. Whether they ran a large boat or small, they were equivalent to captains on seagoing vessels—that is, they held supreme authority. Troublemakers could be bound and held for the sheriff in the next port town, but often the captain dealt with them himself. Some were "taught a lesson," then dumped at the next landing. Some didn't even get to a landing; they were summarily pitched into the water. Or, if they were lucky, the captain pulled the vessel close to the bank where the offender, miserably soaked, could slog ashore through the mud and muck.

You just didn't mess with the boat captains. Like Captain Billy Russell.

His hometown paper, the *Daily Argus* of Crawfordsville, Indiana, liked to write about him. Their May 22, 1894, issue featured an article that told how Captain Billy reacted when one of his passengers lost his bankroll in a gambling den, in the rough and rowdy riverfront section of Natchez called "Under-the-Hill."

Captain Billy marched into the gamblers' hangout and demanded the return of the passenger's money. Of course they just laughed at him. So he marched out, back onto his steamboat, where he hollered, "Okay, you stevedores and roustabouts, drag out our heaviest cable, throw it around that thar building, and snug it up like a lasso. Now cast off!" As the steamship started moving, so did the gambling den, foot by foot, until it was nearly covered with muddy water. Then Billy had the cable undone and neatly stored, and calmly pointed his steamboat down the river.

CHEATERS SOMETIMES WIN: GEORGE DEVOL

The Natchez Under-the-Hill bunch were cheats and sidewinders, but they weren't alone; with easy pickings the boats probably had at least as many crooked gamblers as honest ones. George Devol was one of the most active, and probably the best-known, of the riverboat gamblers—and he was a very accomplished cheater.

Devol rode the steamboats up and down the Mississippi and, as history moved westward, into the Rio Grande, Red, Arkansas, and Missouri Rivers. A big fellow, he liked to fight and particularly liked to butt an opponent with his very hard head (he claimed doctors had told him the skull over his forehead was nearly an inch thick).

George started young, first working as a cabin boy, but soon became a proficient poker player. To give himself an unfailing advantage, he employed marked cards and also carefully stacked decks in advance. Then, along with a generous bribe, he would plant his "new" and sealed decks with the bartender.

Devol also practiced virtually every other method and device of cheating at cards. Of course he would sometimes get caught, and violence often ensued. That's why Devol was always armed with his pistol, "old Betsy Jane," as well as a large knife.

In his *Forty Years a Gambler on the Mississippi*, Devol tells of sailing on the *Sultana* heading for Louisville when a game of five-card draw developed. He joined in, and when it was his turn to deal, went to the bar for a "fresh" deck. Of course he had primed the bartender with several of his own decks, carefully stacked, packed, and then resealed.

With this rogue deck Devol dealt one man three aces, one three kings, and himself four treys. The goal, of course, was to induce the other two to bet and raise vigorously with their good hands while Devol would quietly call all the way to the end. And raise they did, until a very healthy pot was piled in the middle of the table.

At the laydown Devol moaned, "Gentlemen, I guess you have me beat; I only have two pairs." The two opponents ignored Devol as they gloatingly tabled their strong triplets—the aces beating the kings, of course. At that point Devol grinned, "Well, boys, I can top both hands, with my two pairs of threes."

Apparently Devol got away with this antic, but today that kind of "slow-rolling" caper would get at least a good whipping. So, don't try it in home games, and surely not in modern casinos.

Devol's operating philosophy could be summarized as "It's morally wrong to let a sucker keep his money." But Devol did have one soft spot: the clergy. "I caught a preacher once for all his money, his gold spectacles, and his sermons. Then I had some of those queer feelings come over me, so I gave him his sermons and specs back." Kept the money, though. Devol had a soft spot, not a mushy one.

Most of Devol's "career" was spent on riverboats, but he later became alert to the gambling opportunities developing rapidly in the West, and started to follow Horace Greeley's advice. As the West opened up, the opportunities grew: miners, trappers, cowboys, lawmen (almost all of whom loved to gamble), soldiers, train and stagecoach passengers, Indians. Up the Red River to Texas, down the Arkansas "on a stern-wheel boat out of Wichita," every little burg was just an ATM for Devol.

LOTTIE DENO: POKER QUEEN WITH A LOTTA DOUGH

George Devol wasn't the only one branching out from New Orleans and the river.

Carlotta Thompkins began life in Kentucky with a wealthy father who, on business trips to New Orleans, introduced his daughter to the pleasures of gambling. It might seem inappropriate for a young girl to be exposed to the lush betting parlors of New Orleans and the elegant salons of the steamboats, but Carlotta was always protected—early on by her father, and later by her seven-foot-tall black nanny, Mary, who, in the early years, never left Carlotta's side.

Just as well, too, for Carlotta quickly developed a skill at poker, and sometimes a man she had fleeced might become violent. Once a soldier, perhaps disbelieving that such a pretty young lady could actually be good enough at poker to take his entire stack, began to revile her as a cheater. Big Mary yanked the soldier up by his collar, marched him to the boat railing, and cast him overboard.

Like Devol, Carlotta also heard the call of the West and headed for San Antonio, where she discovered a town already two hundred years old and rampant with gambling salons. Carlotta arrived with a flourish and a dramatic persona. A newspaper described her appearance at the Cosmopolitan Saloon: "She created a never-to-be-forgotten picture when she arrived, dressed in the finest style, followed by Mary Poindexter. Mary, being a Negro, was allowed to sit behind Carlotta's chair during the evening (to serve as a lookout), much to the chagrin of Lottie's gambling companions. Carlotta's dexterity in handling the cards soon won her the respect of the biggest gamblers in San Antonio." She was such a good poker player that the University Club hired her as house gambler—essentially a person staked and sponsored by the club, which took a share of her winnings.

With her good looks, hourglass figure, Parisian fashions, and card-dealing dexterity, Carlotta was soon tagged with the sobriquet "Angel of San Antonio." This is where she also received another tag, one that she would embrace for the rest of her life. As the stacks of gold and silver mounted in front of her, a hapless opponent at the table moaned, "Honey, with winnings like them, you ought to call yourself Lotta Dinero."

And she did, shortening it to Lottie Deno for convenience.

Lottie fell in with a companion, but he disappeared after stabbing a man to death. So she took off to search for him throughout Texas, journeying to Fort Concho, Jacksboro, San Angelo, Dennison, Fort Worth, and Fort Griffin. In each town she would play poker until she had fleeced enough players that it became hard to find a game, and then she would move on.

When she strolled into Fort Griffin's Beehive Saloon, that groggery blossomed from a smoky dive into an elegant ballroom. Or so it seemed to the rowdy cowpokes, buffalo hunters, and mule-team drivers, whose heads turned as one to eye Lottie Deno, a true beauty, attired as though for a Parisian salon. The bartender handed her a new deck of cards and she gracefully took her seat at the poker table.

A couple of buffalo hunters and a professional gambler quickly joined her game. Although the buffalo men started with wads of payday money, they were soon busted. The gambler was Doc Holliday, who "daylighted" as a dentist.

Lottie and Doc went heads-up for several hours, until finally Doc stood up with a sigh.

"Well, I guess today is not my day, Miss Deno. Would you care to join me for dinner before my last two dollars are gone?"

"Doc, as I've so often said, I do not join men for dinner—or anything else. Although I am happy to take your money."

"Perhaps you won't object, Miss Deno, if I consider your winnings today as only a temporary loan. Tomorrow is another day, and the cards may run quite differently. Good day to you."

Although Doc seemed calm, inside he was seething. He could stand losses at faro—that game was, after all, mainly luck—but he wasn't used to losing at poker.

Seething would also describe Big Nose Kate, who barged in with smoke pouring from her ears. As Doc's consort, Kate wasn't worried about Doc losing, but she didn't want another woman messing with "her man," and she told Lottie so.

Lottie let 'er have it, verbally. Women in the Old West were every bit the equal of men in their cursing abilities. Though, in substantial contrast to Kate, Lottie appeared to be every inch a lady, her response was direct: "Why you stinkin' slut! If I should step in soft cow manure, I would not even clean my boot on that bastard!" With that Lottie whipped out her derringer, but Doc separated them, and they all lived to play poker and participate in historic gunfights another day.

Lottie vanished all right, but resurfaced with her own gambling room in Kingston, New Mexico, soon adding another in nearby Silver City. As the mining boom ebbed, she moved to Deming with her new husband and bought a liquor distribution business. Their wealth grew, allowing her to become involved in charity work and other civic ventures. Eventually she gave up poker, which had been so good to her, for bridge. While in her later years she was a respected community leader, in her earlier days, in addition to building her own wealth, she had also contributed to the development of the West in several towns.

CHAPTER TWO

Doc Holliday

GEORGE DEVOL WAS A GAMBLER AND A CHEAT. LOTTIE DENO WAS a gambler and a lady. Doc Holliday was a gambler and a gunman—indeed, one of the most intimidating gunmen in the Old West, even if he failed to intimidate Lottie Deno. (Can't win 'em all.)

John H. Holliday was born in 1851 to a wealthy Georgia family. As a kid, he was taught to play poker by an enslaved person owned by his family. He received a fine education, including the study of French, Greek, and Latin, and finished dental school in Philadelphia in the shortest time ever. In Georgia he opened a successful private practice, but soon contracted tuberculosis—the "old consumption," they called it—and moved west. He also started patronizing saloons, drinking and gambling.

Holliday met Mary Katherine Horony, generally known as Big Nose Kate, in Fort Griffin, Texas. Nicknames are often spontaneous, and often unfair. Kate's nose was slightly bulbous in shape: rounded on the tip, not pointed, and not especially big, and something about her appealed to the gambling dentist from the South. Fort Griffin was also where he first met, and became friends with, Wyatt Earp. There Doc gambled full-time, mostly successfully. Wyatt Earp once described him this way:

Doc was a dentist, not a lawman or an assassin, whom necessity had made a gambler; a gentleman whom disease had

*made a frontier vagabond; a philosopher whom life had made
a caustic wit; a long lean ash-blond fellow nearly dead with
consumption, and at the same time the most skillful gambler
and the nerviest, speediest, deadliest man with a six-gun that
I ever knew.*

It was in Fort Griffin that Doc demonstrated the impatience
he had with gamblers and dealers who were not serious about the
game—*his* game. He was playing against Ed Bailey. Bailey had a
tendency to look at others' discards. If you're a poker player, you
know this is among the worst sins you can commit. The discarded
cards are clues to the cards *not* discarded—what the player might
still be holding.

Doc told Bailey once to stop "monkeying with the deadwood."
Then Doc told him twice. Instead of telling him a third time, Doc
just swept the pot. His message was, if you're gonna look at my
discards, I'll just take the pot whether I win it or not.

Now Bailey became self-righteous. He stood, threateningly,
and pulled his gun. Big mistake. Doc was not only unintimidated,
but he might have been basically unintimidatable. He whipped
out his knife and stuck it in Bailey "just below the brisket." Doc
was arrested and confined with a guard in a hotel room.

Once again, enter Big Nose Kate. She followed the deputy
and prisoner to the hotel and casually drifted upstairs to identify
the room in which Doc was being held.

Then she sprang into action. She got two horses and tied
them in back of the hotel. Next, she scouted the hotel, selected
an adjacent shed, checked it out (it contained a horse, which she
released), borrowed a pistol, and set fire to the shed, yelling "Fire!"
In the ensuing melee she dashed upstairs, banged on the door of
the room where Doc was being held, and hollered that the deputy
was needed to fight the fire.

The deputy jerked open the door—right into the face of Kate's
pistol. She took his gun and pitched it to Doc, locked the deputy

in the room, and led the way to the horses. That may have been the moment that caused Doc to attach himself to Big Nose Kate for life.

As his TB worsened, Doc had to give up dentistry—patients wouldn't tolerate the coughing—and he soon turned to full-time gambling. Over in Las Vegas, New Mexico Territory, he opened his own saloon and gambling salon, paying a fine for keeping an illegal gambling hall, although that seemed to be more of a "license fee" than a fine. Doc may have been a mite quick on the trigger, but he was reputed to have a fairly warm personality that attracted friends—when he wasn't shooting them. In Doc's obituary the *Denver Republican* said, "He was a very mild-mannered man, was genial and companionable, and had many excellent qualities."

When Wyatt Earp came to town, the two played poker together. Soon Doc hired Earp to work in his gambling hall. Their friendship grew, and was solidified when, after two men had cornered Wyatt in a saloon and were threatening to kill him, Holliday burst in and saved the day.

Drunks were always a problem. Mike Gordon was a cavalry veteran who was prone to getting loaded and firing his pistol. (He had earlier lost his nose, bitten off by the gambler from whom Gordon was taking money.) One evening his shots were coming too close to people, one going through the pants leg of a bystander and another almost taking out a bartender. These shots evoked a fusillade in return, and Gordon expired. Nobody seemed to know who shot him, so there was no arrest or prosecution, but some time later the *Las Vegas Optic* claimed the shooter was Doc Holliday.

With all this action, the Las Vegas townspeople posted this warning:

All murderers, confidence men, and thieves are hereby notified, that they must either leave this town or conform themselves to the requirements of law. The flow of blood must be stopped and the good citizens have determined to stop it, if they have to hang every violator of the law in this country.

Las Vegas wasn't completely without a functioning justice system. Territorial Supreme Court Chief Justice Kirby Benedict was prone to playing poker in the Exchange Hotel's Buffalo Hall. Someone ratted him out to the grand jury that was considering persons indicted for illegal gambling. When his name was called, Justice Benedict rose from the bench magisterially and responded, "Kirby Benedict enters a plea of guilty, and the court assesses his fine at $10, and what is more, Kirby Benedict will pay that fine."

Holliday and Earp moved on toward the end of 1879, but in 1880 Doc was briefly back in Las Vegas, where he had a long-standing beef with Charlie White. With his doxy Big Nose Kate in tow, Doc stepped off a southbound train, strode into a saloon where Charlie was bartending, and cut loose. As White fell bleeding, Doc gathered up Kate and stepped back onto a train heading southwest. He was needed in Tombstone.

CHAPTER THREE

Poker Rides the Rails

WHILE NEW ORLEANS, SAN ANTONIO, AND SANTA FE DIDN'T need help from gamblers to become famous, nor to attract settlers and investors, other developing Western towns did. Steamboats had substantially answered the demand for transportation, so many rivers, navigable at least by the smaller packet boats, opened up much of the West. But with established cities like Santa Fe, Las Vegas, New Mexico (not that *other* one), San Antonio, Dallas, and others developing throughout the West, there was a need—and of course there was a *marketing* opportunity—for faster and cheaper transportation.

Stagecoaches offered a form of transportation, but the trips were usually long and drearily uncomfortable, as well as expensive. There had to be a better way. And there was, as railroad companies began greedily chasing each other to lay tracks across this vast territory.

The first rail service, then still horse-drawn, started in the United States in 1830. Rail construction was stimulated by completion of the first transcontinental railroad in 1869. Soon westward expansion was a thriving industry, seeing lines competing with each other—sometimes head-to-head, and violently so.

The initial attraction was the large public subsidies to be exacted from each town, which probably explains why villages like Columbus, with fewer than a hundred people on the southern border of

New Mexico Territory, had train service. As towns sprang up and populations increased along the rail lines, the ongoing revenues from ticket sales, freight, and carrying the mail further incentivized railroad expansion. The era of the train had arrived.

Although poker is as portable a game as you can get, playing it on stagecoaches wasn't particularly comfortable, considering there was no proper table, and passengers had to contend with the constant bouncing and wind gusts (there were side curtains, but in warmer months these were rolled up to allow the breeze in). Trains changed that. Passengers had more room, the clacking and rocking didn't disturb the cards, and there were easier opportunities to draw strangers into a game.

As each set of rails was pushed westward, a new town—a "Hell on Wheels"—arose at the end of the line. And in each new town, poker was always present, with professional cardsharps generously willing to help relieve the rail-construction workers of their pay.

When the town had served its purpose as a base for laying tracks, everything was loaded onto flatcars and trundled to the next, newest "Hell on Wheels." The gamblers, bunco artists, saloon-keepers, prostitutes, and some merchants then promptly set up shop all over again. A few of these little burgs went on to become permanent cities, like Cheyenne, Wyoming. It was a muddy railhead until the gamblers came, bringing a degree of fame (or infamy), which in turn attracted settlers, merchants, professionals (lawyers, accountants, real estate brokers), and the media. When the rails moved on, Cheyenne had enough of a start and a presence to continue, growing into today's prosperous city.

As train lines became established, the ultra-wealthy, of the "robber baron" ilk, had private railcars constructed to their specifications, with furnishings approaching those of an Eastern seraglio. Into these charming parlor cars were invited notables and nabobs, and the inevitable amusement was poker. Fortunes were exchanged, and the trains rolled on. (In later days President Truman played poker with Churchill on a train, and even had chips for the game printed with the presidential seal.)

The rails attracted many seasoned gamblers, like George Devol, who may have made his reputation on steamboats but also welcomed the coming of the rails. During the early 1870s he worked the trains between Kansas City, Omaha, and Cheyenne, introducing fellow passengers to the complexities of three-card monte, and plopping down at the nearest poker table when there were no suckers for his shenanigans.

To a substantial degree, the trains opened up the West, populating the new territories with the good and, not insignificantly, the bad, as well as the hopers, searching for riches at the card tables . . . or in the ground. Here and there, small mining strikes were starting to be encouraging.

CHAPTER FOUR

There's a Gold Mine in the Sky, Far Away

GOLD WAS FIRST DISCOVERED IN THE UNITED STATES IN NEW Mexico. Little remembered is the New Mexico mining town of Dolores, in the Ortiz Mountains southeast of Santa Fe, immortalized in James Grafton Rogers's 1912 song "The Town of Old Dolores":

> In the country down below where the little pinons grow,
> It's nearly always half a day to water;
> There stood a little town where the creek come tumbling down
> From the mesa where she surely hadn't oughter.
> The streets were bright with candlelight;
> The whole town joined the chorus;
> And every man in sight let his cattle drift at night,
> Just to mosey to the town of old Dolores.

Dolores, where Thomas Edison was occupied in a gold separation mill for a while, gave us the oldest gold lode mine in the West, the Western song of "Old Dolores," and Dõna Tules.

Who was Dõna Tules? The same words Churchill used to describe Russia could be used for her: She was "a riddle, wrapped in a mystery, inside an enigma." Was she beautiful or ugly? Moral or debauched? A commoner or a lady? Even her name generates questions. Her name at birth was Maria Gertrudis Barceló, but she became known affectionately as Doña Tules, or La Tules. Some say her nickname was derived from the Spanish word for reed, *tule*, because she was very slender; others say it was just an affectionate diminutive of Gertrudis.

Originally known as Maria, this mysterious lady came north to New Mexico Territory in the 1820s with her family, and, perhaps because of her independent and risk-taking attitude, she was quickly attracted to the many gambling opportunities. As gold was discovered in the Ortiz Mountains south of Santa Fe, Maria was there, dealing in the little mining town of Dolores (Real de Dolores de Oro). The town's budget was largely financed by fines or licenses for gambling, and she paid her share. Before long, she was attracted by the greater sophistication and opportunity in nearby Santa Fe. As one biographer described this town, "Governors, judges and other civil officers, who had sworn to uphold the law against gambling, gambled; as did priests, because gambling was not considered a sin and the church had no strictures against it."

Born of nobility in Mexico, as an adult Maria was definitely independent, probably slender, with black hair, dark eyes, and dark complexion. She was possibly "stunningly beautiful"—early on, at least. Later she became less attractive, especially with the constant cigarillo between her lips. But by then she was the wealthiest and most powerful woman in Santa Fe, a status achieved primarily through dealing cards.

Her heritage and literacy entitled her to the honorific *doña*, and she capitalized on it. Continually dealing cards while assiduously managing her money, Maria—now Doña Tules, or simply La Tules—was soon able to purchase a building on Burro Alley just west of the plaza. This she outfitted with elegant furniture, drapery, mirrors, and chandeliers. La Tules then established standards for admission congruent with the opulence of the salon. You couldn't just walk into her Barceló Palace, even with a bag full of gold dust. You had to have the appropriate attire, *and* behavior.

Once inside, however, you were made most welcome, especially by the seductively dressed and comely "evening angels" who were ready to relieve your stress—or whatever—in the bedrooms upstairs. Perhaps the pain of losing a bankroll in the casino was somewhat alleviated this way. In the Barceló Palace big money was often wagered: $10,000, $40,000, $50,000. (In today's dollars, $10,000 would be more than $300,000!)

La Tules may have gained power and wealth, but she also hungered for social standing. In Santa Fe society, La Tules's behavior did not meet upper-class standards—until she spotted an opportunity and quickly embraced it.

Army colonel Alexander Doniphan had been ordered to march toward Mexico, but he lacked the funds to feed his troops. No one would make him a loan, so La Tules provided a thousand dollars, with a single condition: The colonel must escort her on his arm to a formal ball, thus providing her with the desired social standing for polite Santa Fe society.

Whether due to her newfound social standing or an innate sense of propriety, La Tules was firm in enforcing proper behavior within her own family. When her beautiful daughter Rafaela—actually, a stepsister to Tules, although much younger—took a lover, Tules met him with a gun and a priest as he sneaked through a window into Rafaela's room. The marriage was performed on the spot.

Famous she surely was, and a significant actor in the oldest mining town in the West, and later, the social and economic life of Santa Fe in the 1840s. But she also provided prostitutes for the pleasure of her gambling clients, and was quite possibly a tad loose in her personal life.

Claiming close ties to Doña Tules, a few years ago Santa Fe's Palace Restaurant and Saloon included the following legend on its website:

The Palace Saloon is the best surviving representation of the era and atmosphere in which the infamous La Doña Tules held court, and both the powerful and proletariat came to play.

33

There are many stories, truths, half-truths and myths about the powerful and inspirational Doña Maria Gertrudis Barceló, called "La Doña Tules." What is certain is that she ran a very successful gambling establishment (and, perhaps, offered more intimate diversions upstairs) on or near the site of The Palace during the 1840s and early 1850s.

She is said to have had close ties to Manuel Armijo, the last governor of New Mexico under the Mexican Republic, and Archbishop Jean-Baptiste Lamy.

Mystique and history seep from the flocked wallpaper and deep walnut of the Saloon. It's the right spot for pondering the legend of La Doña Tules among good friends and intriguing strangers.

Perhaps the historical connection to La Tules was not the kind of image The Palace wanted to present, because this information no longer appears on its website. But you can still enjoy a drink or dinner at The Palace with the aura of La Tules just around the corner on Burro Alley. Or, you can honor her more concretely by organizing a search party to find her buried gold.

Because, of course, there's a buried treasure story here. La Tules, especially in her later years, handled enormous amounts of gold and silver. The money came from the mines by way of her poker tables, won from miners active in the mountains of New Mexico Territory. There wasn't a bank in Santa Fe until 1870, so she shipped her profits to the United States under the cautious eyes of a cadre of armed guards.

Alas, so the story goes, one such mule team was attacked by banditos, or maybe Comancheros. The guards, faithful to the end (allegedly), hastily buried the gold. And of course, the bandits didn't see this and never searched for it (well, it's a *story*, right?).

So there you are; somewhere between Santa Fe and Independence, Missouri, you may find the "Lost La Tules Treasure" just waiting for you.

THERE'S GOLD IN THEM THAR HILLS

In 1848 California, like New Mexico, was in the uncertain position of transitioning from a Mexican territory to a territory of the United States. And then—Sutter's Mill!

Enthusiastic gold-seekers poured into California, along with their inevitable parasites and freeloaders: professional gamblers, soiled doves, merchants, innkeepers, outlaws, and, of course, always the purveyors of rotgut whiskey. Those coming by ship, either around Cape Horn or with a mule-back passage across Panama, landed in the fledgling San Francisco. First settled in 1776 as Yerba Buena, it was still only a village by the time California was claimed by the United States in 1848.

Gambling dens, saloons, and brothels quickly erupted, populated by miners with their sacks of gold dust, seamen from the hundreds of ships plying the inviting harbor, soldiers and cowboys, leftover Hispanic vaqueros and soldados who chose to stay in the United States because fortunes were being made, and Chinese laborers recruited to work the mines and build the railroads—and who generally loved to gamble. Not to mention a plethora of black-legs, bandits, stagecoach robbers, pirates, and other desperados, all of whom found their way to the infamous Barbary Coast/Waterfront District. Things got so bad that, in 1867, San Francisco instituted America's first "ugly law," which prohibited unsightly people from showing their faces in public. (It has since been repealed.)

Contemporary writers observed that the gambling parlors seldom closed their doors and were constantly crowded with eager suckers at all hours of the day and night. At salons such as the Parker House, Empire, El Dorado, and Bella Union, "Gambling was *the* amusement, *the* grand occupation of many classes, apparently the life and soul of the place. Around the tables the players often stood in lines three or four deep, everyone vying with his neighbor to lay down his money as fast as the cards were turned."

And it wasn't just miners and professional gamblers who were drawn to the gambling halls like moths to a flame. Judges and clergy, physicians and lawyers, tradesmen and mechanics, laborers and farmers—all elbowed their way in to be part of the action. A British artist said gambling in San Francisco was so widespread at the time that even little urchins, ten or twelve years of age, were smoking cigars as big as themselves and strutting about with the air of grown men, as if fully familiar with all the hooks and crooks of that wicked place. They too would bet their money, losing a hundred dollars at a pop.

Housing consisted of crude shacks or tents, disease was rampant, streets were mudholes, and prices were astronomical. Robbery, murder, and kidnapping were commonplace. Seamen were regularly shanghaied, arson and extortion were common, and vicious gangs controlled the town. Eventually the absence of civil government and systematic law enforcement led to vigilante groups exercising severe control.

MADAME MUSTACHE

San Francisco was rowdy, without question. But gambling parlors soon discovered that an attractive female, present as a dealer—or even just a player—went a long way toward calming the rough-and-tumble crowd. That's why the Bella Union employed Madame Simone Jules, an attractive, dark-haired young woman in her twenties. Soon her table was drawing a crowd, with potential gamblers trying to elbow their way in to a seat. When the pushing and shoving produced an angry response, Madame Jules could quiet the would-be combatants with a word and a charming smile.

But then she disappeared, apparently never to be seen again—or was she?

Shortly after Madame Jules's San Francisco disappearance, an attractive young woman stepped down from the stagecoach in Nevada City, east of Sacramento. Miss Eleanore Dumont took a room in a hotel, keeping to herself except to dine—alone—for a week or two. Historians are satisfied that this was Madame Jules, now with a new name.

Soon, Miss Dumont rented a storefront room and opened a card game. Gold miners were welcome, but not if they were profane and disheveled. No, in her parlor men must wear jackets, remove their hats, and swear only in moderation. Above all, they were not allowed to brawl. With her charm and her rules, and the free champagne she provided, her establishment prospered.

One gambler described his 1870s visit:

With several busily occupied tables in the barroom, one on a platform in the middle of the room was vacant—until Miss Dumont descended the stairs, stepped up on the platform, settled herself delicately into a chair, and with a smile invited the surrounding gamblers—all a-stare by now—to join her. As she began to shuffle the cards, two brawny and well-armed characters—her guards—positioned themselves just behind her. As one gambler joined the table, he remarked—with a good deal of bravado—that he intended to either break her or be broken. He was, soon enough, broken.

Nevada City was good while it lasted, but when the mines played out, it was time to find a place where the grass, or at least the cash, was greener. (This practice was repeated throughout the mining towns of the West.) As the mining and accompanying opportunities for profits from a gambling parlor declined, so did the beauty of Eleanore Dumont. She added whiskey and weight—quite a bit of each, in fact—and a fine mustache emerged on her upper lip, resulting in a new and memorable nickname: Madame Mustache.

By 1879 Madame Mustache was running her gambling parlor in the little gold-mining town of Bodie, California, some seventy-five miles south of Lake Tahoe. Her once-famous skill with the cards had deteriorated, and professional gamblers soon broke her bank.

Alone, Madame Mustache walked a mile out of town, drank a bottle of poison, and lay down and died. Although this song by Dave Stamey wasn't written about Eleanore Dumont, it expresses well her sad ending:

Her name was Rosa May,
She arrived one autumn day
To ply her trade in the town of Bodie,
And her cheeks were blazin' red,
From the chilly wind, she said,
But the lines around her mouth were even colder.

They found her a winter's dawn,
The smoke from her fire gone.
Her eyes were open to the endless myst'ry,
And they buried her without prayer
On the slope just over there,
Then they moved along, and were lost to hist'ry.

VIRGINIA CITY, NEVADA

The prospectors, diggers, and panners were crawling over the mountains, and still occasionally finding gold, though not in large quantities. Then, in 1859, the Nevada Comstock Lode was hit. It didn't contain gold, but it did have silver—and *lots* of it. The lode was so big that it started a silver rush, with emigrants from all over the Eastern United States merging with hungry and aggressive miners from San Francisco and Sacramento.

A ramshackle town, Virginia City, quickly developed. One historian described it thus:

Frame shanties, pitched together as if by accident; tents of canvas, of blankets, of brush, of potato-sacks and old shirts, with empty whiskey-barrels for chimneys; smoky hovels of mud and stone; coyote holes in the mountain side forcibly seized and held by men; pits and shafts with smoke issuing from every crevice; piles of goods and rubbish on craggy points, in the hollows, on the rocks, in the mud, in the snow, everywhere, scattered broadcast in pell-mell confusion.

Is it any wonder, in that environment, that miners and seekers sought the (relative) warmth and refuge of the saloon and gambling den? And when a miner made any kind of strike, the place to brag and show off the findings was a saloon. Emboldened after several drinks, the prospector took to the poker tables in an attempt to multiply his strike. The March 1869 *Overland Monthly* described the scene:

> *These club rooms were crowded to their utmost capacity, and the tables were piled with coin and checks, while hundreds of men, who had made lucky strikes at finding, working, or, more frequently, selling mines, were betting away in a single hour what might have kept them, and those dependent on them, for years in comfort, or served as the foundation for a colossal fortune.*

In *Roughing It*, Mark Twain painted a similar picture of this coarse mining town:

> *In addition to the wide-open gambling palaces, there were hurdy-gurdy houses, theatres, brass bands, murders, inquests, riots, a whisky mill every fifteen steps, a dozen breweries and half a dozen jails and some talk of building a church.*

Wouldn't you know it, one of the nicest saloons in Virginia City was established by another lady—an African American woman named Amanda Payne. She provided a striking contrast to the patrons in her Boston Saloon as she glided down the stairs in a fashionable dress with translucent midnight-blue glass buttons. She experienced discrimination in this rip-roaring frontier town, but mostly she was welcomed for offering a more elegant setting in which tired workers and businesspeople could enjoy a cocktail in crystal stemware and dine off bone china, serenaded by classical instrumental music. And of course, they could also relax at the poker table.

Deadwood

Like Madame Mustache and Amanda Payne, Belle Siddons as a youth was stylish and beautiful. Following imprisonment as a Civil War spy, she headed west, changed her name to Madame Vestal, and gambled, vigorously and successfully, against the likes of Wild Bill Hickok, Butch Cassidy, the Sundance Kid, and John Wesley Hardin.

When Deadwood erupted, she changed her name to Lurline Monte Verde and outfitted an omnibus with lush fittings, flaunting lace curtains and an elegant couch with little satin pillows strewn about. In Deadwood she set up her own combination dance hall, gambling parlor, and saloon . . . and fell in love, unfortunately with a stagecoach robber, who was soon hanged. A depressed Lurline turned, like several other Old West women gamblers, to the always-available opium. And, like the others, her beauty, figure, attire, and gambling skills all declined, till she died from some combination or other of opium, alcohol, and cancer.

Deadwood was like other pop-up mining towns in that during the day it was abuzz with the comings and goings of miners having ore assayed or claims recorded, buying the "necessaries" to keep body, and sometimes soul, together, or setting up businesses to suck in the other miners' occasional profits. And by night it was party time. Hard-driving men who had labored during the day for ounces of gold dust were now hell-bent on spending it as quickly as possible on rotgut liquor, prostitutes, gambling, and even the occasional banquet. (Okay, just call it supper, but when celebrating one may be prone to exaggeration.)

Deadwood was on Indian land, which meant it was an illegal settlement. However, the federal government took the position that it had no authority to enforce the law in the area. For quite a while, in fact, there was no locally established law enforcement. It was a place, and surely not the only one in the Old West, where the motto "anything goes" certainly applied. And that *anything* attracted a conglomeration of gamblers and con artists, prostitutes and pickpockets, and a bundle of swindlers ready to capitalize on the enthusiasm of would-be miners who were consequently easy targets for all sorts of land schemes and fake mines. The growing town was filled with yelling and whooping, plenty of gunshots (*mostly* playful), clacks of poker chips and dice, mule-driver shouts, hammering and sawing—a near constant clatter and rattle that inspired Bret Harte in one story to title his town "Roaring Camp."

For many people this exactly describes a place they wouldn't want to be. For Wild Bill Hickok, his buddy Colorado Charley Utter, Hickok's wannabe buddy (or *more* than a buddy, at least in her mind) Calamity Jane, along with Doc Holliday, Madame Mustache, Wyatt Earp, "Bloody Dick" Seymour, Poker Alice, Joseph "White Eye" Anderson, Big Dollie, Dirty Emma, Sizzling Kate, and others, Deadwood Gulch was exactly where they *did* want to be. Why, you could get filthy rich in at least two ways: mining or gambling. Who wouldn't be lured?

CHAPTER FIVE

Wild Bill Hickok

WILD BILL HICKOK WASN'T ALWAYS WILD BILL. HE WAS BORN IN 1837, in Illinois, and christened James Butler Hickok.

As a boy Bill was intensely antislavery. It is said that he and his brother headed to Kansas Territory to join up with other progressive, abolitionist groups. Young Bill got himself a job driving a stagecoach on the Santa Fe and Oregon Trails, where he first met Kit Carson and Buffalo Bill Cody. Then at the age of twenty he was elected constable of Monticello, Kansas.

Though these early experiences in Kansas were not especially notable, they did afford him the opportunity to dip his boot into the gambling waters. And for the rest of his life he was pretty much playing poker when he wasn't shooting—and his shooting sometimes occurred because of a poker game.

How did James Butler Hickok come to be known as Wild Bill? Legend has it that Hickok was in a saloon and when a fight erupted, he jumped up on a table firing his pistol into the air, claiming he'd kill the first man who fired the next shot. The crowd quickly dispersed, and as Hickok was leaving a woman softly whispered, "Good for you, Wild Bill."

It was certainly a better nickname than what he had been saddled with as a youngster. He was then called "Duck Bill" because of his sweeping nose, which had sort of a Richard Nixon / Bob Hope ski-jump shape.

After a couple of years in Kansas, in 1860 Bill drifted up to Nebraska and got on as a stock tender at the Rock Creek Stage and Pony Express Station. He was twenty-three. Although he hadn't yet done anything to create a Wild West "rep," he nevertheless impressed George Ward Nichols, a writer for *Harper's New Monthly Magazine* in 1867. Actually, from this description it might be more accurate to say that Nichols was smitten.

Bill stood six feet and an inch in his bright yellow moccasins. A deerskin shirt, or frock it might be called, hung jauntily over his shoulders, and revealed a chest whose breadth and depth were remarkable. These lungs had had growth in some twenty years of the free air of the Rocky Mountains. His small round waist was girthed by a belt which held two of Colt's navy revolvers. His legs sloped gradually from the compact thigh to the feet, which were small, and turned inward as he walked. There was a singular grace and dignity of carriage about that figure which would have called your attention meet it where you would. The head which crowned it was now covered by a large sombrero, underneath which there shone out a quiet manly face; so gentle is its expression as he greets you as utterly to belie the history of its owner, yet it is not a face to be trifled with. The lips thin and sensitive, the jaw not too square, the cheek bones slightly prominent, a mass of fine dark hair falls below the neck to the shoulders. The eyes, now that you are in friendly intercourse, are as gentle as a woman's. In truth, the woman nature seems prominent throughout, and you would not believe that you were looking into eyes that have pointed the way to death to hundreds of men.

Hundreds of men? Sounds like Mr. Nichols was mesmerized— but this writing was not atypical of the magazine journalism of the time, often looking to build and fascinate readership by "true accounts" that were 90 percent fiction.

Not everyone shared George Nichols's inflated view of Hickok. In particular, David McCanles, owner of the property the Rock Creek station was on, was prone to bad-mouthing him—sometimes calling him Duck Bill and a "hermaphrodite" (wonder if he knew what that was). There was also bad blood between the two over a woman—the age-old story.

So one day McCanles went with two other men to the station, bent on collecting past-due rent. Though the details are debated among historians, it looks like Hickok, who had stayed holed up in the station building while the arguing and cussing went on outside, ambushed and killed McCanles as he entered the building for a glass of water. In the confusion and shooting that followed, three men died (one chopped to death by the stationmaster's wife, with a hoe).

Historians' accounts of the event are interesting, but not as colorful as Hickok's own words, which Nichols quoted directly in another *Harper's* article. (The piece is fascinating but rather long to reproduce here.)

Laying it on, Nichols wrote that Hickok had single-handedly killed nine "desperados, horse-thieves, murderers, and regular cutthroats in the greatest one-man gunfight in history." And during the battle, Hickok, armed with only a pistol, a rifle, and a bowie knife, suffered eleven bullet wounds. (He actually wasn't wounded at all.)

Wild Bill went on, over time, to exaggerate and glorify most other events of his early life, characterizing himself to such an extent that, had he lived instead in the late twentieth century, he would have qualified as a Marvel Comics superhero. The Rock Creek, Nebraska, affair provided the foundation for a lifetime—albeit a fairly short one—of self-aggrandizement.

Not long after the Nebraska episode, the Civil War erupted and Bill enlisted in the Union Army, first as a teamster and then as a wagonmaster. That didn't last long—he was discharged in less than a year. But he hung around Missouri employed as a wagonmaster, and *possibly* as a Union spy in Confederate territory.

HICKOK THE LAWMAN

After the war "Wild Bill" got on as a policeman in Springfield, Missouri; he also ran for election as city marshal, but lost, with only 27 percent of the vote. He spent much of his time playing poker, and evidently sought to present himself as something of a tough guy. It's probably safe to say that Hickok seems to have been consciously acting out a role for much of his life.

His image in Springfield, as described by the local newspaper, was as a "ruffian, a drunken, swaggering fellow, who delighted when 'on a spree' to frighten nervous men and timid women." Bill was prone to riding his horse into saloons, stores, and hotels and having the horse perform tricks. Some seem to have been enchanted by these performances, although the proprietors, less so.

One favorite haunt was Springfield's Southern Hotel, already nearly a hundred years old. Bill enjoyed the magnificent old architecture and furnishings, but he enjoyed the games in the poker room more. His poker opponents included a soon-to-be-famous George Armstrong Custer, as well as Davis Tutt, against whom Hickok often played and who wouldn't live to become famous.

One evening Hickok was playing with three businessmen and was up about $30 when Tutt strolled in and joined Bill's table. The two were not friends; in fact, they nurtured a mutual antagonism. Hickok had been a Union soldier, and spied against the South. Tutt had been a Confederate soldier, and the recent surrender still rankled in his veins. Besides that, they were both "stuck on" a pretty young thing who seemed to delight in vixenishly playing one against the other. In the Old West, killings occurred for much less important causes.

Now Bill started losing, and soon had all his money in the pot; in the showdown Tutt turned over three kings against Bill's three jacks. As Tutt raked in the money, he reminded Bill that he was still owed from a loan back in Arkansas. They argued over the amount of that debt, and since Bill was now broke, Tutt reached down and picked up the fine pocket watch Bill always kept on top of his cards.

"I'll just take this fine timepiece for security," Tutt said with a smirk as he slid the watch into his vest. Hickok had warned Tutt before not to touch his watch, so this was really rubbing salt into the wound. He glared at Tutt coldly: "Don't you be flaunting my watch. If you do I'll kill you."

Tutt laughed in Hickok's face, then strolled out with Bill's watch *and* his money.

Next day Tutt, showing unwise bravado, came swashbuckling down the middle of the street wearing the watch. Hickok stepped out into the road and hollered, "I warned you, Tutt!" They both stopped, then drew. Tutt's shot missed; Hickok's hit Tutt dead center. (Allegedly at seventy-five yards; some witnesses said it was a scratch—i.e., lucky—shot, since Hickok at this point did not have a reputation as a crack shot.)

Thus the foundation was laid for any number of future *High Noon* movie shoot-outs.

Hickok was arrested for murder, but the jury acquitted him after the judge delivered this instruction:

> *That when danger is threatened and impending a man is not compelled to stand with his arms folded until it is too late to offer successful resistance and if the jury believe from the evidence that Tutt was a fighting character and a dangerous man and that defendant was aware such was his character and that Tutt at the time he was shot by the defendant was advancing on him with a drawn pistol and that Tutt had previously made threats of personal injury to defendant . . . and that defendant shot Tutt to prevent the threatened impending injury [then] the jury will acquit.*

As with the Nebraska incident, Hickok, when interviewed by *Harper's New Monthly Magazine*, continued to exaggerate his "reputation," saying, "Yes, Wild Bill with his own hands has killed hundreds of men. At the Wilme Creek [apparently Wilson's Creek] fight in the Civil War, I had fired more than fifty cartridges, and I think fetched my man every time." Though a master of self-promotion, Hickok seems to have served as a role model for other famous, or would-be-famous, gunslingers in the Old West, such as Billy the Kid, Wyatt Earp, Calamity Jane, and John Wesley Hardin.

Hickok was soon appointed a deputy United States marshal, captured some army deserters and mule thieves in Kansas, scouted for Custer, and ran for election as sheriff of Ellsworth County, and then as marshal, but lost both races. Throughout these years he continued to play poker; according to Joseph Rosa, Bill's biographer, "Sometimes, he sat for hours under the glare of a smoky lamp in the company of the officers and men at Fort Sidney, gambling."

Hickok finally won an election in 1869 to be sheriff of Ellis County, Kansas, the home of Hays City and Fort Hays. Bill soon killed three men—in the line of duty, one could say, although he did seem to be quick on the trigger.

For the third killing, Hickok was essentially protecting himself as he was jumped (in a saloon, of course) by a passel of vengeful troopers from the nearby fort. Although pinned to the floor, he managed to get one of his pistols into service and shoot the man on top of him through the wrist. The trooper understandably relaxed his hold enough that Bill was able to put another bullet through his belly. After wounding one more trooper, Wild Bill made a wild plunge through a glass window and disappeared.

Bill went back to scouting for the Seventh Cavalry, sustaining himself with poker at every juncture. In 1871 an offer of a job as US marshal in Abilene, Kansas, drew Bill in off the trail and back to being an officer of the law. His misadventures in Abilene, along with movement of the railroads farther west, soon led to Bill's dismissal.

By 1872 Wild Bill was in Georgetown, Colorado, out of a job, and spending his time at the poker tables. The next year, he was hired by Buffalo Bill Cody to tour with him and "Texas Jack" Omohundro in Cody's show, *Scouts of the Plains*. At this point Hickok's skill as an actor was evidently not well developed. In one scene the three men are supposed to be swapping yarns and downing slugs of whiskey. When the bottle was first passed to Bill, he took one slug and promptly spewed it into the wings, roaring, "Cold teas don't count—either get real whiskey or I ain't tellin' my story!" From then on he got 100-proof, but the tea-and-spewing bit was retained through every performance.

During the tour Hickok often cautioned Cody about the perils of gambling, especially with the risk of expert sharpers and stacked decks. He advised that when you play against a stacked deck, make sure you've got a hand to beat theirs—and he touched his hand to his pistol.

Bill's gambling presence was occasionally mentioned in local newspapers; the *Junction City Union* noted in 1876 that Hickok ran his own "saloon and gambling hell" there, and he was also reported to frequent Colonel Jamison's gambling rooms in Leavenworth.

As the train tracks extended west, new towns, as temporary locations for stocking construction supplies, hiring workers, bookkeeping and the like, were created. These were wide-open, lawless places (as noted earlier, they were commonly called "Hells on Wheels"), and Cheyenne was exemplary, packed with "gambling halls, saloons, dance halls, variety theaters, and whorehouses." This image evidently appealed to men like Wild Bill, who were seeking opportunities that might otherwise be discouraged by men with badges.

According to G. R. Williamson in *Frontier Gambling*, Bill soon had an encounter with the famous Mississippi riverboat gambler George Devol. This time Devol came out second best:

[In Cheyenne's Gold Room Saloon] a tall, longhaired man wearing a pair of blue-tinted spectacles and a hat pulled down low on his head made his way to Devol's faro layout and placed a $50 bet. The stranger lost his bet and then promptly

*laid a second $50 bet on another card, which won. When
Devol pushed over $25 to cover the win the man growled a
protest. Devol pointed to a sign that stated "the house limit's 25 dollars." The man furiously replied, "But you took fifty
when I lost." Standing his ground the dealer shot back, "Fifty
goes when you lose." The dealer's words were barely out of his
mouth when the stranger struck him and his partner over the
head with his walking stick. He then upended the faro table
and took all the money that hit the floor. Stuffing the money
into his coat, he pulled two long-barreled Colt revolvers and
backed his way out of the saloon. As he left the room, his hat
flew off, revealing a shoulder-length mass of sandy hair, and it
was then that Devol realized that the stranger was none other
than the legendary James Butler "Wild Bill" Hickok.*

Although mining was also on Bill's mind, poker was foremost,
and Cheyenne afforded him all the poker play he could want. It
also afforded him a wife. On March 5, 1876, James Butler Hickok
married Agnes Lake, a woman then world-renowned for her earlier career as a tightrope walker, lion tamer, and equestrian. The
newlyweds took the train to Cincinnati to visit her family. After
a short visit Bill returned to the West while Agnes stayed to help
her daughter care for a new baby.

South Dakota was opening up, offering even better poker and
mining opportunities than Cheyenne. So in mid-July, 1876, that's
where Bill headed—to Deadwood Gulch, possibly drawn by the
romantic-sounding name.

In terms of culture and refinement Deadwood was about the
bottom of the barrel, a lawless burg whose denizens were among
the toughest and meanest in the Old West. But with Hays City,
Abilene, and Cheyenne behind him Wild Bill wasn't much concerned about what he considered routine violence. His reputation,
exaggerated though it may have been, was sufficient protection
against the ordinary toughs.

Of course, his reputation was also a draw for the would-be gunslingers who might figure killing Wild Bill Hickok would earn them untold renown. For such as these, he was always on the lookout. Unfortunately, his eyes diminished the strength of his lookout, as Bill was losing his sight. Watching him in Deadwood, his pal Joseph "White Eye" Anderson observed that Hickok was a dead shot at twenty-five paces. But at greater distances, or when daylight began to dim, he was half-blind.

Bill's presence in Deadwood was not welcomed by all. The ones who had crooked ways of relieving miners and gamblers of their gold dust and dollars were concerned that Hickok, a famous ex-lawman who had "cleaned up" Hays City and Abilene, might become marshal of Deadwood and then their games would be pretty well up. Some believe that, as Bill spent his days in Deadwood peacefully playing poker, there were crooked gamblers conspiring to have him killed.

Evidently unaware of any such plotting, Bill continued to visit the gambling dens, his favorite game being five-card draw. As biographer Joseph Rosa wrote, "At every opportunity Wild Bill gambled, but he did not make a fortune at it. In his last days it is evident that he lost more than he won." Even Bill freely admitted that he was much less successful with cards than he was with his pistols.

Bill's deteriorating eyesight would not have been much of a factor in his poker playing. The dominant game was five-card draw; in this game vision is practically irrelevant since players do not see any cards other than their own until the showdown after all betting has ended. Less common by this time was five-card stud, a game in which, progressively, four of each player's five cards are dealt faceup. But poker protocol would call for players to keep all of their exposed cards clearly visible on the table, so good eyesight wasn't essential, and bad eyesight would have been at worst merely an inconvenience.

Bill was in Deadwood only about twenty days. He was reported to have spent his nights—at least, the later hours of them—in a canvas-covered wagon, while his days were invariably at the poker table in one or another saloon. There are reports of extraordinary gunfights—but without a trace of documentation—and no reports of his going to the mines.

As described in the opening chapter, Hickok strode into Nuttall & Mann's No. 10 saloon just after noon on August 2, 1876. Though he couldn't get the seat he wanted, with his back to the wall, he still sat down.

And that's how Jack McCall was able to get behind him. Hickok evidently didn't notice McCall, but commented to the table on the hand he had just lost, "The old duffer, he beat me on the hand." Then came McCall's loud curse as he shot Hickok in the head.

Thus his hand of aces and eights entered the folklore of the Old West, to be known henceforth and eternally as the "dead man's hand."

Was this really Hickok's hand? There is no proof, no documentation, and plenty of doubt. But does it matter? Whether he held aces and eights or anything else, the legend will continue.

Hickok was inducted into the Poker Hall of Fame in 1979, nearly one hundred years after he passed away, allegedly for his legendary poker-playing abilities and his dedication to the game—although I suspect it was mostly due to his giving us the most famous poker hand in history..

Dying at the age of thirty-nine, Hickok would not have met the minimum age requirement of forty instituted some time after his induction (this requirement was passed because public balloting kept pushing then-twenty-three-year-old Tom Dwan—a shame, because Dwan was, and still is, a much better poker player).

CHAPTER SIX

Calamity Jane

In Deadwood, Bill's girlfriend was Miss Calamity Jane. At least, that was the role she tried to play—not that Bill welcomed her attention, or ever did more than bemusedly tolerate it. But this didn't cause Calamity a moment's pause; she portrayed herself as allied with Hickok even after he was killed, and carried it off to the degree that she actually was engaged by a touring company to tell her tale.

The Calamity Jane story is a crackling good one. Of course, it's not all true, but you could say that about the tales of a number of famous Westerners.

Martha Jane Canary was born in 1856, to Robert Canary and his young wife Charlotte. Things appeared to start out okay, since the family owned a 180-acre farm in Missouri. But neighbors characterized Robert as lackadaisical and inept as a farmer, while Charlotte was behaving much like an older Martha/Calamity, favoring questionable men, hard liquor, cigars, and loud swearing.

Within weeks of the death of Robert's father, his siblings and other kin were filing legal claims against Robert over the inherited assets. Robert and Charlotte were hauled into court, but the record shows that they "appeared not"—as they had quickly decamped for the West.

On the difficult journey, the need for food afforded Martha Jane opportunities to practice her shooting as well as to become a strong rider. She would need these skills, because Charlotte contracted pneumonia and died, and shortly after arriving in Utah Robert also died, leaving Martha and her siblings orphaned.

As was the custom of the day, the three children were "farmed out" to different families. Martha soon struck out on her own, turning to prostitution; she was about fourteen.

For the next several years Martha Jane wandered the Northwest, usually tagging along with an exploring expedition or a military unit. In her personal account (less truth than fiction) she claimed that she scouted for General Custer; swam the Platte River; then, wet and cold, she rode ninety miles with a military dispatch, which got her hospitalized for fourteen days. She also claimed that she was a Pony Express rider on the "most dangerous leg of the route"—that she'd followed a stage under attack by Indians, taking over when she found the driver was dead and driving to the nearest stage station, where she unloaded the baggage and then jumped back in the seat and drove "right through the Indians," delivering six passengers and the dead driver to Deadwood.

We do know that she "stowed away" on the Dodge/Jenney expedition into the Black Hills from Fort Laramie in May 1875, but she was discovered and ejected, a process "repeated daily during the whole trip." Such tenacity, and for what end? Surely not just for the food that soldiers might sneak to her. No, her goal—assuming she had planned it out and wasn't just acting thoughtlessly—was most likely for male companionship, plus the pleasure of "getting away" with something.

Martha Jane's stowaway act was repeated numerous times. Sometimes she dressed and passed as a soldier—until her ineptitude in presenting a poorly formed salute drew snickers from real soldiers. (In spite of the efforts of drill sergeants everywhere, "poorly formed" salutes are pretty rampant, especially from civilians trying to present themselves in a quasi-military role, such as various commanders in chief—American presidents.)

Sometime during all of these escapades, our female adventurer was branded "Calamity Jane."

Wherever Jane went, she played poker. If you're unemployed and you like to be with men, the saloon with its card tables would have been, in the Old West, your best opportunity. The only unusual thing about this was that Calamity was, of course, a woman—although perhaps not terribly unusual at that, as we've seen there were a number of women poker players throughout the West. In that country most men gambled because it was pretty much the leading legitimate recreation around. Town leaders might try to outlaw it; they also tried to outlaw prostitution, and wearing guns in town. These efforts were strikingly unsuccessful mostly because the miners, soldiers, cowboys, trappers, professional gamblers, and professional prostitutes collectively and consistently ignored the new laws. Poker, after all, was how they passed the time on the trail, in camp, during any breaks. They just didn't see it as sinful.

(This scofflaw attitude continued until the end of the twentieth century. Poker was illegal in just about every jurisdiction in the United States, except Las Vegas and Atlantic City, and yet it was still played all over the country. After I started playing seriously in 1992 I could always find a game, in Texas, Kansas, Kentucky, District of Columbia—just about everywhere. Then as the poker craze erupted and grew, fed by the telegenic World Series of Poker, more and more legal casinos, often associated with Indian reservations, appeared. Today I live in New Mexico, within a twenty-minute drive of four casino poker parlors.)

By 1876 Calamity Jane was known throughout the Northwest. Indeed, her nickname had been spread by then-popular print media throughout the country. In some ways Jane was bigger than life. She usually dressed in men's frontier work clothing: buckskins, boots, wide-brimmed hat, weapons crammed into her belt. She was boisterous and profane, and carried herself with confidence, even arrogance. Her skin was darkened and leathery. On the trail she carried a supply of "bug juice," and would frequently take a slug. Consequently, she was often drunk, and more so when she was settled in a saloon or at a poker table. All this meant that she was pretty easy pickings at poker, but it *was* a way to be in among "the boys."

Unadvisedly she continued to gamble even as her losses mounted. Drunks often enough get grandiose ideas of their poker-playing prowess, and this malady probably affected Calamity as well. And, lacking other means of support, she may have been hoping that poker would afford her a nominal income. It didn't—even if she did manage to win occasionally.

Calamity's penchant for telling tall stories, usually some fiction or exaggeration about her own life, would sometimes enchant or at least distract other players to the point where she could win some hands that were otherwise losers.

Calamity probably thought she had won big when she joined the wagon train that Wild Bill Hickok was helping lead into Deadwood. She promptly homed in on Bill. Although he had told his new wife, now back in Ohio, that he was going to Dakota for gold mining, he actually spent most of his time (in the twenty days he was there) in saloons, at the poker tables. According to biographer Rosa, he found plenty of other diversions: "He consorted with prostitutes, whom he rarely trusted; gambled incessantly; and consumed whiskey in large quantities but never got drunk." And, where Bill went, Calamity went—insofar as she could and insofar as he would tolerate her.

Tolerate is the most accurate word for their relationship. In later life Calamity told a different story. She said they were lovers, they married, she bore his children, his death was unbearable. Hickok became a major part of Jane's manufactured life story. But in reality? As Gertrude Stein would say, "There was no *there* there." Wild Bill didn't want to be Calamity's boyfriend, nor her lover, nor her husband. But as long as she was just joining him at the poker table—well, anyone can join the game.

Then Hickok was murdered, in the most infamous poker game in history. In her autobiography Calamity was of course the heroine, though in wrenching grief, as she went after the murderer Jack McCall with a meat cleaver (presumably having left her gun on her bed), captured him, and brought him to justice. (In truth, McCall was captured—though not by Calamity—tried and promptly acquitted, and then tried later in a more legally established court, found guilty, and hanged.)

With the addition of the imaginary Hickok relationship Calamity's star soared. She was featured in a dime novel and cited in various books and newspapers. Her character was a major figure in the play *Drama of Life in the Black Hills*. And she starred on stages throughout the East and Midwest as "The Famous Woman Scout of the Wild West! Heroine of a Thousand Thrilling Adventures! The Terror of Evildoers in the Black Hills! The Comrade of Buffalo Bill and Wild Bill!"

In 1885 she married Clinton Burk, thus becoming Mrs. Martha Burk. (My wife's name is also Martha Burk, though she's better-looking and -behaved than Calamity.) Then Calamity married again, and again, had children, drank excessively, wound up in a county poorhouse, and moaned, "Why don't the sons of bitches leave me alone and let me go to hell my own route?"

For all the roughness of her life and the falsity of her stories, one truth of Calamity is perpetual, and voiced by just about everyone who knew her: She was kind to the sick, to the down-and-out. During a smallpox epidemic she was often the only one who would sit without fear beside victims and wipe their faces with a cool rag, giving them water and comfort. She would sacrifice her own well-being and her usually pitifully small belongings to help anyone who needed it—a sort of tough-looking, tough-talking Florence Nightingale of the Western plains.

Photos of Calamity usually show a coarse woman in buckskin or men's work clothing, not the least bit refined. But one picture with Bill Cody, probably taken when she was a late teen, shows a fairly handsome woman in ladylike clothes, one who undoubtedly would have been called "beautiful" in a land of so few women.

In 1903 Calamity Jane died. She was buried in Deadwood's Mount Moriah Cemetery *next to Wild Bill Hickok*—her final fantasy, her final wish. Their graves are visited by thousands, and marked by empty whiskey bottles and playing cards left as mementos.

Calamity Jane wanted a life of adventure and glory. That wasn't her real life. So, in the best Old West tradition, she made it up—just like some of our cowboy "heroes" did in places like Abilene, Kansas.

CHAPTER SEVEN

Abilene: The Cowboy Era Begins

ABILENE, KANSAS, WAS A DINKY LITTLE STAGECOACH STATION when the Kansas Pacific Railroad extended a line westward in 1867. Then Joe McCoy saw an economic opportunity: Here's a rail line connecting to Chicago with its big meatpackers, and down there in south Texas is a bunch of beef, on the hoof, ranging in the brush country with no nearby market.

So McCoy built a hotel in Abilene, called it the Drover's Cottage, and sent messengers to south Texas with flyers that encouraged Texas drovers to drive their cattle north to Abilene. They were told they could follow an established trail that had earlier been laid out by Indian trader Jesse Chisholm (not to be confused with New Mexico cattle baron John Chisum). The flyers claimed the route was easy, with friendly Indians, good grazing all the way, and no difficult hills or rivers.

And the cattle drovers came—first with a few head, and then many thousands: 350,000 by 1869.

Each herd came with a dozen or so cowboys, cowboys who had eaten the same meals, typically just twice a day, and hadn't touched a drop of liquor (it was often severely prohibited by the trail boss), spoken to a woman, or had a chance to run free and whoop and holler for two months or more. But they had played poker, as Andy Adams describes in his *The Log of a Cowboy*: "As soon as supper was over and the first guard had taken the herd, the poker game opened, each man being given ten beans for chips. . . . . As wood was plentiful, we had a good fire, and this with the aid of the cook's lantern gave an abundance of light. We unrolled a bed to serve as a table, sat down on it Indian fashion, and as fast as one seat was vacated there was a man ready to fill it, for we were impatient for our turns in the game." These cowboys got all their pay at the end of the trail, and came to town full of spit and vinegar looking for a bath, shave, haircut, hat, new clothes, and then, excitement.

They started at the saloons for hard liquor, with some in their early teens experiencing their first taste. Then they were off to the bordellos, followed by more liquor, gambling (with generally quick and thorough losses), and unbounded rowdyism. Abilene came alive with the fusillade of gunshots, boisterous yelling and singing, inevitable fights, the racing of horses up and down the dirt-packed main street—and occasionally into saloons and stores. Older cowpunchers were likely to be Civil War veterans from the Confederate side; they disdained efforts by local sheriffs and marshals—who they viewed as Yankees, whether they had served with the Union or not—to rein them in and especially to disarm them.

Of all the saloons in Abilene, the Alamo was probably the finest. From the hitching post out front, three glass double doors led into a long room with a bar on the right that featured a giant mirror, brass fittings, and nude paintings. The rest of the room was filled with gambling tables, and to the rear an orchestra seemed to play constantly.

Abilene was booming economically but was also a rough place to live. In order to corral the cowboys, the town leaders appointed a succession of law officers. First were two policemen from St. Louis; they lasted less than one day. Then came Tom "Bear River" Smith. Although Smith carried a gun, and used it occasionally, he mostly relied on his fists to maintain control and to enforce the "no guns within town limits" ordinance.

Smith was, understandably, not popular with the cowboys. He survived two assassination attempts, but was finally killed in an ambush outside of town. So a new marshal was appointed: Wild Bill Hickok.

Wild Bill's gambling propensity was well known to the Abilene town leaders, and they simply assured him that he would have ample time to indulge what was at least a passionate pastime and may have been an obsession. According to his Abilene friend, Charles Gross, "He would gamble the shirt off his back." But Bill's eyes weren't on gambling opportunities alone; he recognized that Abilene was already a rough town that would require strong measures by the marshal to enforce the law.

In Abilene, with his standing now as town marshal, Wild Bill began to dress publicly as he did later as a performer in Buffalo Bill's shows. He grew his hair long until it hung to his shoulders, topped with an unusually wide-brimmed black hat with flat crown. Now his usual costume included a long Prince Albert coat, boiled white shirt under an elegant brocaded vest, flowing red sash around his waist, and trousers tucked into his boots—which were of the finest calfskin and custom-made. This was not the attire of a man who just grabbed the first shirt out of the wardrobe. His clothing defined his persona, especially with the two always-present ivory-handled pistols worn butt-first.

Professional gamblers in the Old West dressed similarly, as had the pros during the steamboat days. Like the modern opera singer Maria Callas was prone to say, "Ya gotta have a *look*." Bill had a look, and it helped to advance his fame nearly as much as his deeds.

Before the cattle herds started to arrive, Hickok was occupied with routine duties: strengthening the jail and rounding up stray dogs (at fifty cents each). But from a population of only five hundred in April, the town had mushroomed to seven thousand by June—and Bill's hands were full.

His gambling haunts were one of his concerns. He broke up cheating whenever he spotted it, made professional gamblers move their tables out of the dark areas into the light, and protected drunks by stopping a game when he saw that someone had consumed too much alcohol.

The town council had passed an ordinance barring the carrying of guns in town, giving Hickok and his two deputies plenty of work and making them the enemy of the Texas cowboys. Jesse James was one such piece of work; John Wesley Hardin, who at age eighteen had already killed several men, another.

Besides dealing with trigger-happy and whiskey-infused cowboys, Bill was moving against the "undesirables" of Abilene. His progress was reported in the *Abilene Chronicle*:

> *For the last ten or twelve days almost every train eastward-bound has carried away and relieved this community of vast numbers of sinful humanity. Prostitutes, "pimps," gamblers, "cappers," and others of like ilk, finding their several nefarious avocations no longer remunerative or appreciated in this neighborhood, are embracing their earliest possible convenience, by hook (mostly by hook) and by crook, to obtain the necessary wherewithal with which to secure passage to Newton, Kansas City, or St. Louis.*

Given Abilene's continuing reputation, the editor may have been engaging in wishful thinking.

All was certainly not serene one night in October, as a mob of rowdy, drunken cowboys were making the most of their last few days in town. In front of the Alamo, a rowdy named Phil Coe—with a reputation as one mean hombre—fired into the air. Hickok heard from across the street and demanded to know who had fired the shot. Coe smirkingly said it was him, shooting at a stray dog. So Wild Bill pulled his two navy revolvers and ordered all guns turned in. When Coe moved toward him with guns drawn instead, Bill shot him with both pistols.

Then Hickok, whose eyesight had been deteriorating for years, sensed movement to his side; he whirled and shot an innocent bystander, who also happened to be his friend. A tragic mistake. A couple of months later the town council dismissed Wild Bill. Their decision may have been over these and other killings, or it may have been because of the decline of the cattle trade—the railroads were now reaching to Ellsworth, Newton, Wichita, and other new Kansas cowtowns.

NEWTON

You may not have heard of Newton. No one ever made a movie about this Kansas town, so in our culture it almost doesn't exist. But the shoot-out in Newton on August 20, 1871, claimed more lives than the so-called "Gunfight at the O.K. Corral." As author Charles L. Convis once said, "They called it the Newton General Massacre, and it began with a poker game."

The Atchison, Topeka and Santa Fe extended its rails into Newton in July of 1871. And Newton, one could say, made the most of its short period of infamy. By the end of the first season, Newton's image and reputation were so ablaze that it was described as "the wickedest city in the West." It already offered twenty-seven saloons and eight gambling dens, with eighty professional gamblers running them. The *Emporia News* reported that "the town is largely inhabited by prostitutes, gamblers and whisky-sellers. Pistol shooting is the common amusement. All the frequenters of the saloons, gambling dens and houses of ill fame are armed at all times, mostly with two pistols."

Harry Sinclair Drago would later write, "There are different shades of depravity. Newton got the blackest scum that would not have been tolerated in Abilene and Ellsworth even in their wildest days."

The "action" was concentrated in an area called Hide (sometimes Hyde) Park, allegedly because "the girls showed so much of their hide." Besides cowboys and others seeking excitement, Hide Park attracted outlaws and professional gamblers.

The notorious John Wesley Hardin came up the Chisholm Trail with a cattle drive and found Newton's poker tables hospitable. Hardin was a professional gambler and could have been called a professional killer, except he mostly killed for his own satisfaction and not as an agent for others.

The gamblers and saloon-keepers quickly figured out that the overheated and under-policed atmosphere was, as they often say in Texas, "bad for bidness." So they assessed themselves a "license tax" and hired a constable and a deputy sheriff. First to be hired was the two-fisted Irishman and habitual gambler, big Mike McCluskie. McCluskie had a toady, an eighteen-year-old lad named Jim Riley he had found in a railroad car dying of tuberculosis. McCluskie took him under his wing, got him some new clothes, and helped with food and spending money. Naturally the kid adored McCluskie, following him on his rounds.

Young Riley also liked to play poker whenever he had a little money. One night he was in a five-card-draw game with Bill Bailey (yes, there *was* a Bill Bailey), a hard-drinking, troublemaking Texas cowboy, doing the dealing. When asked how many cards he wanted, Riley choked back a hacking cough and said "Two." Bailey took three cards.

Riley bet ten; Bailey raised him twenty. After some hesitation, Riley pushed in fifty dollars in chips.

McCluskie grabbed Riley's chips. "What are you doing, Mike?" Riley asked.

"Saving you some money, kid. Bailey's dealing from the bottom of the deck."

In accordance with the Western code of honor, Bailey yelled, "You're a damned liar!" and reached for his pistol. But he was already staring down the barrel of McCluskie's gun. When the cards were turned over, Bailey indeed had four aces against Riley's four kings. This incident, of course, made enemies of Bailey and McCluskie (and Riley was so grateful that he swore off gambling altogether).

That night a drunken Bailey ambushed McCluskie and missed, but Mike's shot bored through Bailey's heart.

A few nights later McCluskie dropped by Tuttle's saloon to play cards, Riley following along. A passel of cowboys came in led by Hugh Anderson, a onetime ally of John Wesley Hardin, with several killings in his past. Anderson walked up behind McCluskie at the card table and, yelling "You are a cowardly son of a bitch!," shot him in the back of the head—portending the killing of Wild Bill Hickok by several years.

Anderson hadn't paid any attention to the tubercular kid in a shadowy corner. He should have. The kid wore a pair of six-guns, although no one there had ever heard of him using them. He used them that night, however, and with a vengeance. He blasted away until his guns were empty, then turned and walked out the door—never to be seen or heard from again.

He left five dead plus Bailey and McCluskie, and seven others wounded. They shoulda made a movie.

WICHITA AND DELANO

They did make a movie about nearby Wichita. Filmed in 1955, *Wichita* starred Joel McCrea in the totally fictitious role of Wyatt Earp cleaning up the town, but critics liked it.

By the time the trains came, Wichita was already a developed town. It had started as a trading post on Jesse Chisholm's route into the Indian Territories, and was incorporated in 1870.

Wichita was helped along by some bold ladies. Catherine McCarty, with her companion William Antrim and sons Josie and Henry (who would later be known as Billy the Kid), homesteaded in the Wichita area and was the sole woman signatory on the town charter. And there was Texan Margaret Borland, a trail boss who led her own herd of a thousand head up the Chisholm Trail to Wichita from south Texas.

When the trail herds and cowboys started arriving, they were welcomed at first. But soon things got out of hand, and

Wichita instituted strict policing. That just encouraged the gamblers, saloon-keepers, and prostitutes to decamp across the river into an unincorporated area called Delano. Here there were no restrictions on gun carrying or carousing. And here the leading saloon and "bawdy" house was run by Rowdy Joe Lowe and his wife (or "wife"—couples in the Old West often dispensed with formalities), Rowdy Kate.

With their poker tables and saloon, Joe and Kate made a lot of money from the enterprise, but this attracted "Red" Beard to open a competing establishment only fifty feet away. He did okay, until a soldier shot one of his women. Red opened fire on the soldiers, which of course angered them, so that night they burned his place down. This was just fine with Rowdy Joe, who picked up Beard's business while the building was being reconstructed.

Joe's reaction galled Beard, and the more he drank the galled-er (I know; it's not a word, but I like it) he got, until he decided to take a shot at Rowdy Joe through the window of his saloon. A gunfight ensued—highly predictable. Joe and Red missed each other, but a stray shot hit a bystander in the head and killed him.

Beard was not satisfied. After more alcohol, he went looking for Joe. Joe saw Red first, ambushed and shot him from behind (not the way Gary Cooper did it in the movies), and that sort of ended the feud. Several months later Joe was found not guilty after a short trial (self-defense?).

Delano wasn't *all* about killing. During 1872–1873 cowboys loaded saloon girls and prostitutes into wagons (it's possible that the cowboys and girls were also—ahem—loaded) and took them down the river a short distance. The "doves" would then strip down to nothing, and when the pistol was fired they would race back to the saloons, whooping and hollering. (You may not believe this, but for the 150th anniversary of the Chisholm Trail in 2017, the Delano Historic District scheduled a reenactment of the Running of the Doves by saloon girls. Sorry, I don't have pictures.)

Beyond Wichita and Delano the rail lines extended to Caldwell, where the city marshal Henry Brown and his deputy took off to a neighboring town and robbed the bank. They forgot to take off their badges. They were lynched.

CHAPTER EIGHT

Wyatt Earp

Besides Wild Bill Hickok, the person most likely to pop up in the Kansas cowtowns was Wyatt Earp.

Earp is difficult to profile; his biography keeps overshadowing other, more-reliable sources. *Wyatt Earp: Frontier Marshal* by Stuart Lake was published in 1931. It was largely based on interviews with an elderly Wyatt, who died before Lake was finished, and substantially fleshed out from Lake's own imagination. The accuracy of Lake's writing (or lack thereof) doesn't seem to matter; later books and movies, including several about the fight near Tombstone's O.K. Corral, have been based on the book's fantasies without qualification or question, evidently following movie director John Ford's recommendation: "When the legend becomes fact, print the legend."

Earp was born in 1848 in Illinois. His family was comprised of his older brothers Newton, James, and Virgil, younger brothers Morgan and Warren, and sisters Virginia, Adelia, and Martha. Soon after Wyatt's birth, the Earps moved to Iowa, and eventually to Lamar, Missouri.

Wyatt was elected constable of Lamar, having run against his brother Newton (the two may have colluded in order to discourage anyone else from entering the race). In 1871 Wyatt was accused by a citizen of overcharging for official services and keeping the extra money. So he moved on, and was then arrested and indicted for stealing horses in the Indian Territory. Wyatt lit out, escaping from jail before the trial began, and never again showed his face in that territory.

At one point Wyatt was listed as living in Peoria, Illinois, according to that town's *City Directory*. There he was arrested and fined—twice—"for being in a house of ill fame," a house he was not only visiting but lived in, as the *Directory* shows. (A minor debate in *True West* magazine focuses on whether Wyatt was a pimp, with the argument essentially over the definition of "pimp.")

Earp supposedly then spent time in Ellsworth, Kansas. The town had the usual cattle and cowboys, and with them, gamblers and hooligans—men like Ben and Billy Thompson, whose time in Ellsworth was marked by a killing that began with a poker dispute. By the time Billy got to Ellsworth he had already killed a soldier in an Austin whorehouse, plus an eighteen-year-old boy, and Ben had allegedly killed a man in a knife fight.

The Thompsons came to Ellsworth and set themselves up as house gamblers in Joe Brennan's saloon. One day Ben introduced professional gambler John Sterling to a high-stakes poker game, with the understanding that Ben would get a percentage of Sterling's winnings. However, Sterling won big and ignored Thompson. Ben went looking for Sterling, and they got into an argument. When brother Billy heard and came a-running, he ended up accidentally shooting the sheriff, who had stepped in to break up the argument.

Billy got a horse and hightailed it out of town, leaving a tense situation still boiling in Ellsworth. Brother Ben was arrested for "felonious assault with a deadly weapon," but was soon released. And that was it.

But not for Wyatt Earp's gullible biographer, Stuart Lake. He said Wyatt, a youthful bystander, stepped up to the mayor and casually suggested that if *he* was sheriff he'd clean house. The mayor fired the entire police force and pinned a badge on Earp. Wyatt calmly walked across the street in the face of Ben

Thompson's shotgun and hundreds of angry Texas cowboys and ordered Thompson to throw down his gun. And Thompson did.

What a hero. In swallowing this story, Lake said it established Earp as "the all-time greatest marshal in the West, and in general a faultless and invincible superman."

Problem is, it never happened. There's no evidence, not even a mention, in the *Ellsworth Reporter* or anywhere else, of Wyatt Earp being in Ellsworth—and an event like Lake described would have been big news in the demonstrative and effusive newspapers of the Old West.

By 1874 Earp was in Wichita, trying to find work while making a bit of money gambling. He helped the police track down thieves who had stolen a man's wagon, and this probably got him hired under Marshal William Smith as a part-time policeman and city maintenance man.

Alas, two days after starting as a policeman Wyatt was in jail, under arrest for roughing up a hotel proprietor. Once released, he probably did a credible job as a policeman, although he did have a penchant for pistol-whipping. And he loved the ladies. This could interfere with his duty of collecting license money from the brothels, especially since Bessie and Sallie Earp were fee-paying prostitutes. Bessie was reputed to be Wyatt's sister-in-law, the wife of his brother James. Sallie was an old "friend" going back to Peoria days.

Wyatt did improve his reputation with his gentle treatment of a drunk: The *Wichita Weekly Beacon* reported that he had found the drunk passed out on the street with $500 in his pocket. Instead of taking the drunk's money, Earp sobered him up and helped him get home.

Wyatt noted later in life that "us old-time shootists knew to always leave an empty chamber in our pistol so the hammer can't accidentally catch on something and fire a bullet." He must have forgotten that rule on January 9, 1876. He was in a poker game in the rear of Wichita's Custom House saloon, rocking back on the hind legs of his chair, when his pistol slipped out of his coat pocket, hit the floor, discharged, and sent a .45 caliber slug through his coat.

Wyatt and Bat Masterson had run into each other before, and renewed their acquaintance in Wichita. They both liked poker and would often be at the table together. Their friendship later extended through Dodge City and Tombstone.

In his biography Earp is quoted as claiming that he received a telegram from the mayor of Dodge City, to the effect that "You've cleaned up Wichita; now come and clean up Dodge."

Wyatt Earp left Wichita for Dodge City in 1876, of his own volition (but not with a telegraphic encouragement from the mayor of Dodge, as Earp claimed). He was probably going to join brother Jim, who was running a thriving bordello. In spite of Wyatt's record in Wichita, Dodge hired him as deputy marshal. During the slow part of the season, after the cattle herds had been sold and loaded onto trains bound for Chicago and the cowboys had left, local law officers had little to do. Some would take off for several months to hunt buffalo, try some prospecting, or ride the gamblers' circuit. In 1877 Wyatt joined them on this circuit, which had grown to roughly cover the West from San Francisco through Denver, Kansas City, Omaha, Tucson, Hot Springs, Arkansas, and the Texas towns of Austin, San Antonio, Fort Worth, and Dallas. He ended up back in Dodge City.

Wyatt seemed to mature in Dodge. No longer the boy who had been in trouble in Illinois, Missouri, and Indian Territory—not to mention Wichita—he seemed to have more self-confidence than before, was less prone to drawing his gun for shooting and more likely to settle things against a misbehaver by "buffaloing" (the term then used for whacking someone over the head with a pistol). He even sometimes jailed town officials that he suspected of violating the law. His reputation grew accordingly, and newspapers like the *Dodge City Times* were quite complimentary toward him.

By late 1879 the cattle drives to and through Dodge City were mostly history, few cowboys were around, and good poker games were harder to find. Earp started looking for more-active towns, since the cattle towns had dried up and the "Hell on Wheels" railheads were pretty much no more. The trains had traversed the West long enough that most rail stops had matured into civilized towns. It was time to move from cowtowns to mining towns, where the miners would periodically amble into town with a bag of gold dust to be weighed—and, often enough, staked at a poker table.

Wyatt first headed for Mobeetie, Texas, where he was run out of town for a swindle, then to Las Vegas, New Mexico, where his friend Doc Holliday had a saloon and gambling parlor. Heading further west, Earp rented a house in Tombstone with his brothers and began looking for silver. He had tried to start a stage line but found there were already two others operating, so he sold his. He got on with Wells Fargo, riding shotgun on company stagecoaches, and then joined his brother as a deputy US marshal; both were working under the actual federal marshal, who was 250 miles away. As a law officer Wyatt was described as calm, determined, fearless, and not excitable.

A would-be miner and try-to-be gambler named Michael O'Rourke was such a hopeful five-card-stud poker player that it was said he would bet when he had nothing better than a two-spot (a deuce) as his hole card. Thus he became known as "Johnny-Behind-the-Deuce." One day Michael/Johnny was playing in Quinn's Saloon over in nearby Charleston. An engineer from a local mill got up from his table to cash in, having lost a fortune in the all-night game. As he left the table he called Johnny a cheater. Of course Johnny went for his gun at the "insult." So did the engineer, but he was a bit slow, and died from a bullet to the chest.

The engineer was well-liked in Charleston; Johnny, much less so. The citizens got in an uproar and there was noise of a hanging. The local lawman, wisely deciding he was no match for a mob with guns, loaded Johnny in his wagon and beat it to nearby Tombstone. With the mob howling at his heels, the lawman with

Johnny in tow crashed into the Oriental Saloon, where fate that day had placed Wyatt Earp.

Earp quickly grabbed a scattergun just as the mob rode up. Pointing both barrels at the leaders, he said, "Boys, don't do anything foolish. The price you'll pay won't be worth that tinhorn." The Charleston sheriff and two Tombstone lawmen were then able to spirit Johnny away to what was supposed to be a more-secure jail in Tucson. But it couldn't hold Johnny-Behind-the-Deuce; he escaped, and was never heard of again.

With this impressive showing, Earp was brought on board at the Oriental Saloon as a partner. His responsibility was to "police" the premises, and in particular, to rein in Johnny Tyler. Tyler was a local bully who, with his buddies, was continuously raising a ruckus in the Oriental with the obvious intention of driving other patrons away. (Tyler may have been sponsored by competitive gambling interests, or just seeking an ownership share in the Oriental for himself.)

By this time Earp had something of a reputation, what with the Johnny-Behind-the-Deuce episode plus the drama of his Dodge City days, so he was able to intimidate Tyler into staying out of the Oriental. Tombstone then hired Wyatt as a police officer in 1880.

The next year brought the famous O.K. Corral shoot-out, but we'll get to that later, in the Tombstone chapter.

An appeal from Luke Short in Dodge City took Wyatt back to Kansas, to join Short, Bat Masterson, and several other noted gunmen for the "Dodge City War," which of course developed over gambling—but more on that later, as well.

Eventually Earp roamed the West, passing through San Francisco, Idaho, San Diego, El Paso, Denver, Alaska, Seattle, Tonopah (Nevada), and Los Angeles. Wherever he went, he would open a saloon or run a gambling operation; eventually, these left him moderately rich.

Wyatt Earp died in 1929 at the age of eighty.

CHAPTER NINE

Bat Masterson

Wyatt Earp was good friends with Bat Masterson, in Wichita and later. Masterson was a gambler and a gunman, but as good as he was (or at least his reputation was) with a gun, he was even better as a poker player.

Born in 1853 and christened Bartholomew, not William Barclay as he later signed his name, by the time he was eighteen Bat Masterson had made his way to the Dodge City area to work with his brother Ed on a grading contract with the Santa Fe Railroad. He soon became a buffalo hunter. The buffalo camps gave young Bat his introductory lessons in poker, for whenever two or more men sat down for a few minutes to rest, a deck of cards was likely to appear.

At its simplest, poker is an easy, fun game where you just hope for good cards and bet 'em when you get 'em. But when the game involves experienced players, your money will be gone before the learning gets started. To continue to play in even these unorganized games, Bat had to learn quickly or quit. And not playing anymore wasn't really acceptable, for then you were shut out of the primary social activity of the crews on the hunt. The answer—Bat's answer—had to be to play conservatively, husband your scarce money, and watch and learn from the other players.

That strategy gives the neophyte a chance to learn or intuit something about odds and probabilities. He gets to watch other players' faces and match their play against the cards they eventually show down. If he is diligent and has reasonable intelligence, he should soon begin to limit his losses, even winning some pots through his own skill and not just from good cards.

Bat Masterson committed himself early on to becoming a serious poker player. In time he became a professional and made his living with cards. Guns were only an adjunct, albeit a necessary one.

Bat and brother Ed landed in a tent town called Buffalo City which, as streets were platted, was renamed Dodge City after the nearby fort. Bat soon graduated from skinner to hunter. Buffalo hunting (one could almost call it harvesting) was similar to the development of the Western cattle trade in that the animals were running free. As with cattle herds, it took a crew to do all of the work: hunters to shoot the beasts, and others to skin the carcasses, peg out the hides to dry, and rough-butcher the meat. The hides and meat (mostly hams and tongues) could then be sold, and settlers would later roam the hunting grounds to harvest the bleached bones, which were valuable for making fertilizer.

With word in 1874 that the buffalo were running strong in the Texas Panhandle, a group of hunters including Masterson headed south from Dodge. They set about constructing modest buildings, including a saloon and restaurant, near the crumbling remains of an old Indian trading post called Adobe Walls.

That year the buffalo were slow to start their northern migration, so the company played poker and practiced their shooting while they waited. When the buffalo came, the killing started, including the killing of hunters; small groups began coming back into camp with reports that Indians had ambushed members of their parties. The smell of war was in the air. Some retreated back to Dodge, but nearly thirty, including Masterson, were determined to stay for the buffalo.

Then one day in June, 1874, the attack came. Over two hundred Kiowa, Comanche, and Cheyenne charged out of the morning sun, their loose alliance signifying an intent for a big war. The Indians evidently expected to overrun the camp on the first pass, but the hunters were experienced in the use of their big Sharps rifles. Many Indians fell, and they pulled back to regroup. The hunters had suffered only two casualties, men who had been still asleep in their wagons when attacked.

The Indians made repeated attacks over the next several days, but eventually word got around to other camps and, during a lull, supportive hunters came drifting in. As the hunters' side grew to over a hundred, the Indians quietly left, leaving the original company free to make it back to Dodge City. With the potential Indian threat now preventing any serious buffalo hunting, Dodge City settled down to serious gambling, drinking, and fun.

But then more adventure called. General Nelson Miles was given orders to form an Indian Territory Expedition to "subdue the hostiles" operating in the Texas Panhandle and Indian Territory (now Oklahoma). Bat quickly volunteered. Each man's marksmanship was tested, and Masterson excelled.

In the meantime, the crude camp the hunters had constructed near Adobe Walls was growing, and now included corrals, lodging establishments, mercantiles, and of course more and more saloons, gambling rooms, and bordellos. It would later be called Mobeetie. Once Bat's military stint was up he went back to hunting buffalo, but eventually he spent more and more time enjoying the gambling in Mobeetie.

One day Bat was in the Lady Gay dance hall entertaining (or vice versa) Miss Mollie Braman. This angered an army sergeant named King who was "stuck on" Miss Mollie; he drew his gun, confronted Bat and Mollie, and shot them both. Though wounded, Bat returned fire, and soon Sergeant King, along with Mollie, lay dead. It took several weeks under a doctor's treatment before Bat was back in the saddle.

Returning to Dodge City, Masterson was hired as undersheriff with Sheriff Charles Bassett. But gambling fever ran strong in

Bat's veins, and the stories he was hearing about Cheyenne were a powerful draw. So he took leave of Dodge and headed north, hit a hot streak at the poker tables that lasted five weeks, then took his winnings and struck back for Dodge City, where he was promptly elected sheriff.

In this capacity he rode with Bill Tilghman, Marshal Charlie Bassett, and Wyatt Earp in a posse that brought down James Kenedy, the killer of variety actress Dora Hand (accidentally, he said—he was trying to kill the mayor, who was then out of town). Kenedy's father was a wealthy cattle king who had already used his wealth to buy his son's way out of jail over a shooting in Ellsworth, and he did it again in Dodge. Some things never seem to change.

With the cattle trade season coming up, Bat invested in the Lone Star Dancehall in partnership with Ben Springer. This was one of the classy establishments, praised in the *Dodge City Times* as "gorgeously arrayed" and "tastefully ornamented." Doesn't sound like the sort of place where there would be violence, or card cheats.

Ah, but it was still a bar, and cowboys would still be cowboys. As noted Texas author Charlie Siringo told the story in *A Lone Star Cowboy*:

> I drew my pay . . . to celebrate the glorious Fourth of July in the toughest cattle town on earth. That celebration came near to costing me my life in a free-for-all in the Lone Star Dancehall, in charge of the now noted Bat Masterson. The hall was jammed full of free-and-easy girls, longhaired buffalo-hunters, and wild and woolly cowboys. In the mixup my cowboy chum, Wess Adams, was severely stabbed by a buffalo hunter. Adams had started the fight to show the longhaired buffalo-hunters they were not in the cowboy class. . . . A town marshal tried to arrest us, but we ran him to cover in an alley, then went out of town yelling and shooting off our pistols.

Much in the mode of Wild Bill Hickok, Masterson appreci-
ated the need to have a "look," and thus dressed stylishly in suit
and tie. He usually sported a bowler/derby-style hat with rolled
brim, a hat that was common except when Texas cowboys, with
wide-brimmed hats close to sombreros, came to town. In photos
Bat's bowler is worn at a cocky angle. The image of Bat Masterson
portrayed in movies and television series, with colorful brocaded
vest and gold-tipped cane, may be a modest exaggeration for commercial consumption. Although he was given a gold-headed cane
in 1885 when he was named the most popular man in Dodge City,
no photo exists of him with it.

In 1878, Bat's brother Jim Masterson and Wyatt Earp were
appointed deputy city marshals under Charlie Bassett; the next
year Bat donned the additional badge of deputy US marshal. (City
marshal was a town appointment and US marshal was a federal
appointment.) The big buffalo hunts were now dwindling, but the
cattle herds and cowboys still came in droves each summer. Even
so, with all this firepower on the side of the law, there was plenty of
time for Bat and Wyatt to attend to their first love: poker.

Bat Masterson's biographer, Robert DeArment, says that this
period gave Dodge City a new title. In addition to being known as
the "Queen of the Cowtowns," it now added the moniker "Mistress of the Gamblers." The gamblers were there in force; in addition to Masterson and Earp, DeArment reports the gambling
tables hosted the likes of Ben and Billy Thompson, Mysterious
Dave Mather, Wyatt's brothers Virgil and Morgan, Rowdy Joe
Lowe, Dick Clark, Luke Short, and Doc Holliday.

Bat played with and against most of these gamblers, and
reportedly did not embarrass himself. As a lawman he of course
was called on frequently to deal with conflicts at the gambling
tables and in the saloons, and along the way he probably made
his share of enemies—a large-enough share, anyway, to lead to his
defeat when he ran for reelection as sheriff.

The substantial reduction in Bat Masterson's law enforcement responsibilities left him mainly in the role of professional gambler. That was fine with him. Playing poker full-time was more fun and certainly more lucrative than "sheriffing," and he didn't have to risk his life dealing with other people's conflicts.

CHAPTER TEN

Dodge City

In western Kansas, Dodge City stood ready to welcome the gamblers and cowboys with open arms—and open gambling halls, open saloons, and open bordellos.

Even as Dodge grew, the more-refined element saw that the town's economy depended so heavily on the cattle herds that it would be better to contain the roughness than to ban it. So the rule became, "Anything goes, south of Front Street."

In the popular mind, Dodge City was a continuously boisterous town with shoot-outs and killings every day. In fact, like Abilene, Wichita, and even Tombstone, the violence that made the news and a town's reputation was rather rare. (Dodge averaged about three killings a year from 1870 to 1885.) But because it could be so dramatic, violence tended to be emphasized in the media of the day, and subsequently in books, movies, and song. Dramatization also turned the occasional shooter into a larger-than-life badass gunslinger—which always sold newspapers and magazines.

The everyday doings of these towns was generally pretty calm. During the day saloons were mostly social gathering places where you could enjoy a free lunch and a beer, run into several friends, and always find a game of poker. Poker games, like any gambling activity where the stakes can run high, could occasionally erupt into violence: fistfights, knifings, shootings. But in the main they were quiet and the players were routinely well-behaved. Of course such behavior doesn't make news or a history that is publicized. So the characters that we think of today as big-time lawmen, outlaws, and gunfighters often spent a part of most days casually playing poker. That certainly was what occupied Wyatt Earp, Doc Holliday, Wild Bill Hickok, Bat Masterson, Luke Short, and others of fame, much more than the part-time duties of the typical marshal, sheriff, or constable.

Even before the cowboys came, Dodge City, at first called Buffalo City, had a reputation as a gambling and carousing mecca with buffalo hunters and soldiers from nearby Fort Dodge. As early as 1872 Henry Raymond, who hunted buffalo with the Mastersons, would write in his diary:

> It was just showing signs of the arrival of a new day, and, seeing a light across the street—there was but one street [Front Street, along the Santa Fe tracks] open on one side—I wended my way to this light. In entering there appeared a card-table with men around it; and on the table were stacks of poker chips and piles of money indicating that the game had been going on all night. The man with his back to me as I entered wore a blouse and protruding below it were the barrels of two large revolvers. I learned later this was Bill Brooks. Quite an unusual sight for a tenderfoot!

And then when, as author and working cowboy Teddy Blue put it, "we pointed them north," by 1875 *north* came to mean heading for Dodge, forsaking Caldwell and Wichita.

By this time an ordinance had already been adopted making it illegal to carry a gun north of the Santa Fe tracks. Cowboys were to take their guns from their holsters and deposit them at Robert Wright's store. Wright, later mayor of Dodge City, observed that the stack of pistols sometimes amounted to more than a hundred.

The ordinance didn't apply south of the Santa Fe tracks, and even if it had it probably wouldn't have restricted the early populating of the local boot hill. The first killing was of an innocent black man who was purposely shot by a gambler named Denver. Years afterward Denver bragged about the killing, said he did it just to see his victim kick.

The coming of the cowboys produced a significant expansion in "entertainment" facilities: saloons, comedy theaters, bordellos, and billiard parlors. According to entertainer Eddie Foy, the Comique Theater itself was noisy with the clack and clatter of poker chips, cards, balls, dice, and other wagering paraphernalia.

Gamblers were involved in a killing at Tom Sherman's dance hall when they got into it with some soldiers from Fort Dodge. Card conflicts sometimes spilled out over the whole table or the entire gambling salon, and in this case "three or four," to quote mayor Robert Wright, were killed and several wounded. Wright says that in 1872 it almost seemed like there was "a man for breakfast" every day.

As for Dodge's reputation in those early days, Wright quotes the *Hays City Sentinel*:

> *After a long day's ride in the scorching sun, I arrived in Dodge City. Dodge is the Deadwood of Kansas. Her incorporate limits are the rendezvous of all the unemployed scalawags in seven states. Her principal business is polygamy without the sanction of religion, her code of morals is the honor of thieves, and decency she knows not. In short, she is an exaggerated frontier town, and all her consistences [sic] are operated on the same principle. . . . The employment of many citizens is gambling. Her virtue is prostitution and her beverage is whisky. . . . Seventeen saloons furnish inspiration and many people become inspired, not to say drunk. Every facility is afforded for the exercise of conviviality, and no restriction is placed on licentiousness. The town is full of prostitutes and every other place is a brothel.*

Early on, Dodge City leaders decided to not outlaw gambling, prostitution, or alcohol; banning the carrying of weapons was as far as they thought they should go. They knew that the buffalo hunters, cowboys, freighters, and gamblers needed a little room, just as long as they weren't shooting up the town.

To maintain order, they went for a who's who of experienced gunmen as law officers. Over several years these included Bat, Ed, and Jim Masterson; Bill Tilghman; Mysterious Dave Mather; Wyatt Earp; and several less-famous but fully competent gunsels (to use a "modern" term). These fellows had to deal with the likes of Doc Holliday, Clay Allison, Luke Short, and even some of their fellow lawmen when they got liquored up, or simply riled up.

In the mining towns individuals would ride their donkeys to town with a sack of gold dust—to buy provisions, yes, but also to drink, gamble, and become acquainted with a few ladies. In Dodge, they would find a plethora of saloons designed to draw them in.

Once inside they invariably partook of a variety of mood modifiers: beer, fancy cocktails, old-fashioned rotgut (a common version was called Taos Lightning, and might be composed of a mixture of whiskey, water, gunpowder, rattlesnake heads, red pepper, and chewing tobacco—sometimes already chewed). With spirits thus elevated, the next stop would either be the prostitutes' rooms upstairs or the noisy, exciting gambling tables. Even the most modest establishment had room for a table or two of poker or faro.

On the upper end of the scale were the more-elegant establishments, such as Dodge City's Long Branch; for several years Luke Short was part owner. The Long Branch featured a five-piece orchestra and served, ahem, sarsaparilla—honestly. And milk, lemonade, and tea. But hard stuff, including elegant cocktails, also was served over the ornate mahogany bar. As nice as the Long Branch was, violence could still erupt—it *was* the Old West, after all, and poker is by definition a contest, a challenge, a *battle*.

Into such an establishment one evening walked former Kansas governor Thomas Carney, now a wealthy businessman who fancied himself quite a poker player. He soon attracted three other "businessmen" for a social game—not aware that his opponents were actually professional gamblers. As the game wore on, continuous imbibing produced a looser atmosphere, and stakes were raised substantially.

In those days poker and its rules were evolving (that continues today, of course). The straight flush was not yet recognized, leaving four aces or four kings with an ace as top hands. (Obviously if one hand holds an ace, no one else can have four aces.) One further quirk: The deck included a joker (also called a "cuter"—not "cutter") that could be counted as an ace. The joker and the ace of spades looked somewhat similar, especially to one already both inebriated and excited.

And so it came to pass that the ex-governor was dealt a hand of four kings and the cuter, which he misread as the ace of spades. So he thinks he has an unbeatable hand. The raising begins; Carney pushes the pot ever higher, eventually adding his gold watch and chain. Then comes the showdown. Carney is nearly panting with anticipation of this substantial pot of riches. But there on the table is spread a hand of four real aces. Carney's hand is second best—a loser.

The former governor slowly pulled himself up from the table. Head bowed, he shuffled out of the saloon and to the train station, where he pulled himself up on an eastbound freight. He looked so sad and pitiful that the trainman didn't have the heart to throw him off.

CHAPTER ELEVEN

Luke Short and the Dodge City War

LUKE SHORT WAS THE WRITER OF WESTERN SHORT STORIES AND of books *Blood on the Moon*, *The Branded Man*, and *Trumpets West!* This is not about him. This is about the other Luke Short, probably the basis for the novelist's pen name.

Our Luke Short, the occasional Old West gunfighter and constant gambler, was from Arkansas, where he was born in 1854. He had no formal education, but according to Bat Masterson he was an exceptionally well-read man by the time of his death. "He could write an excellent letter; always used good English when talking and could quote Shakespeare, Byron, Goldsmith and Longfellow better and more accurately than most scholars."

But he could also ride and rope well enough to become a cowboy at the age of fifteen. Later during his tenure as an army scout—when, at least according to Bat Masterson, he killed six Sioux—Luke served so honorably that the *Fort Worth Daily Gazette* called him "the bravest scout in the government employ." Still, the army arrested him for selling liquor to Indians. Short escaped the army, made his way to Leadville, Colorado, and quickly became entranced with the gambling scene.

Legend has it that Luke, before he had been in Leadville long, had a run-in with a known bad man, a man with a "reputation" who was considerably bigger. Call him Mac.

Luke had placed his bet at a faro layout, and Mac was messing with Luke's chips. Luke asked him politely to take his hands off his chips. Mac started to get nasty, said he would mess with any $%#"+* chips he wanted to, and just what did little Luke plan to do about it ("little Luke" was only about five feet six).

The dealer, who was familiar with Mac's reputation, became agitated, tried to softly intervene, and said he would make the amount of the bet good to avoid a quarrel.

"You won't make anything good for me," Luke said. "That's my bet and I won't let anyone mess with it."

Mac, who was used to people stepping aside for him, grew livid. "You little runt. If you try to reach your hand for that bet I'll shoot your $%#"+* hand off."

Luke reached for the bet, Mac reached for his gun—but it was too late. Luke had drawn, shoved his pistol into Mac's face, and let fly. Luckily for all, I guess, the bullet went through the cheek and Mac was not killed. Of course, the sheriff called it self-defense and didn't bother Luke.

This probably established a precedent in Luke Short's mind: If challenged, act first and act fast. Because of his diminutive size, challengers likely expected him to capitulate and thus weren't quite ready for his quick response—a response that his friend Bat Masterson characterized as being like "lightning."

Things developed quickly and well for Luke. His instant reputation made people respect him and avoid getting into a confrontation. His warm personality easily made him friends, and the combination of a "rep" and a friendly personality made the saloonkeepers anxious to have him at their tables. In keeping with his new standing, Luke began dressing in tailor-made suits, modeled after the better class of gambling men.

Like many Western gamblers, Short got itchy feet even though he was doing well, and in 1880 he moved on to Kansas City. His stay there was brief. He was accused of swindling a man in three-card monte (of course *every* game of three-card monte was/is a swindle), and was jailed briefly.

Enough of Kansas City; Tombstone, in the person of Wyatt Earp, was calling. As noted earlier, Earp had been brought into the Oriental Saloon partnership to quiet things down, but he figured he needed help. So he recruited Short and Bat Masterson as dealers.

It was off to Arizona Territory, where Short didn't exactly calm things down. One evening he was dealing faro when a drunken Charley Storms, frustrated over his losses during the night, took a swing at him. Storms apparently saw Short as an "insignificant little fellow." Knowing of his pal Short's facility with a pistol and his constant readiness to use it, Bat Masterson stepped between them. He then led Storms outside, instructing him to go to his room and sleep it off.

Masterson and Short then stepped outside and were talking when Storms came storming (sorry) up (he had not gone to his room after all). He grabbed Short by the arm and drew his .45 Colt with the taunt, "Are you as good a man as you were this morning?"

Short broke away while unlimbering his own pistol and shot Storms twice. Holstering his gun, he murmured, "Every bit as good."

He left Tombstone in April 1881, well before the O.K. Corral imbroglio. He stopped off in Deming, New Mexico, to see what kind of gambling the miners were up to, but Dodge City opportunities were calling.

Back in Dodge, Short bought into the Long Branch Saloon in partnership with William Harris. They decided they needed to encourage the gamblers a bit, so they added a "coterie of singers."

In the next election Harris ran for mayor, with Lawrence Deger running against him. Things were looking good for Harris until the night before the election, when the construction trains of the Santa Fe railroad brought in men picked up from different locations along the line. The next morning the men were all on hand and obtained control of the election board by filling vacancies, closely following the provisions of the law. They then voted Deger in.

The new mayor and city council passed an ordinance outlawing prostitution. The Long Branch was immediately raided and three of the women arrested. When Short discovered that no prostitutes had been arrested from the other saloons, he smelled a rat. This led to an argument between Short and a policeman; gunfire was exchanged, although no one was hurt. But Short was arrested, jailed, escorted to the train depot, and directed to either go east or go west, but to stay out of Dodge.

So Luke went east, back to Kansas City. First he looked up Charlie Bassett at the Marble Hall Saloon; Bassett was an old friend and former sheriff. They lined up Wyatt Earp, Bat Masterson, Doc Holliday, "Rowdy Joe" Lowe, and Shotgun Collins, and let the word spread that they were headed for Dodge—ready for the "Dodge City War."

Seems like when he saw the crew Luke had assembled, the mayor had a wee change of heart. As Short and his compadres began arriving in town, no longer was he persona non grata. Ol' buddy Luke was welcomed like a long-lost citizen. This is how Bat Masterson described the reception:

> I never met a more gracious lot of people in my life. They all seemed favorably disposed, and hailed the return of Short and his friends with exultant joy. I have been unable as yet to find a single individual who participated with the crowd that forced him to leave here at first. I have conversed with a great many and they are unanimous in their expression of love for Short, both as a man and a good citizen. They say that he is gentlemanly, courteous and unostentatious.

Not a shot was fired—the so-called "war" had ended with a whimper. The Long Branch reopened, the cowboys and gamblers were happy, and peace was restored upon the prairie.

But, the times they were a-changin'. Short and Harris sold the Long Branch to new owners toward the end of the year, with

Short joining up with Bat Masterson for more-lucrative gambling opportunities in Texas.

Dodge's days as a cattle town were likewise winding down. Severe droughts in the West were followed by two of the bitterest winters ever known, with blizzards that showed no mercy. When the spring of 1887 arrived, three-quarters of the cattle on the open ranges were dead. Though there were still ranches and stockmen, the days of the cowboy celebrated in film and song, along with the cattle trails and cowtowns and slick gamblers, were essentially over.

After a visit to San Antonio, Short moved to Fort Worth and bought into the White Elephant gambling house. This establishment became one of the largest in the Southwest and made Luke a lot of money, but he also spent—and gave away—a lot. His good nature made him an easy touch, especially for gamblers who had just gone broke at his tables.

But his good nature wasn't an asset with Jim Courtright, a man-killer who was feared by practically everyone. He leaned on Short to hire him as a special officer for the White Elephant. Luke had befriended Courtright in the past, but this time he told him his presence in the place would so intimidate people that it would seriously drive away business, saying, "I'd rather just pay you a good salary to stay away completely."

Luke told Bat Masterson about the troubles with Courtright while they were sitting in the billiard room: "I tried to reason with him, but he is not a reasonable man. I'm afraid he still has a grudge." While they were talking, one of Luke's employees came in and told him Courtright was out front and wanted to see him. Short said, Sure, tell him to come on back here. The employee said Courtright had already refused to come back; he wanted Short to come out.

So Short went out front, and he could see by Courtright's angry demeanor and the pair of pistols he was wearing that this visit wasn't about palaver. Both men apparently drew at the same time, but Short was faster. By the time Courtright hit the floor, Luke had placed five bullets in his angry body.

> The little man's hands were like lightning
> The bad forty-four was the same
> The forty-four spoke and it sent lead and smoke
> And seventeen inches of flame.
> —"Mister Shorty," Marty Robbins

Investigators concluded that Courtright drew first but Short was quicker. The grand jury thus refused to indict, calling it a case of justifiable homicide—a departure from the usual conclusion of self-defense.

CHAPTER TWELVE

Tombstone

How do you top Deadwood for an unappealing town name? With Tombstone, of course.

Founded in 1879, Tombstone was a bit late to the party. But it quickly caught—nay, surpassed—the others in infamy.

Ed Schieffelin's 1879 discovery of silver in southern Arizona Territory brought the prospectors—along with gamblers, saloon-keepers, prostitutes, etc., etc.—a-running, and the new town of Tombstone arose amid the cacti and caliche. Naturally, Tombstone adhered to the established template for mining towns: first tents and shacks and whiskey dipped from barrels, saloons of rough-cut lumber following, eventually a jail, general stores, hotels, and actual homes. Within two years there were 110 saloons, most with gambling tables or rooms, and an additional 14 separate gambling dens.

Initially law enforcement wasn't even a recognized term, but with a preponderance of tough customers and a fair share of bandits, the need became clear soon enough. In the gambling scene a dispute soon developed, reaching the point where it threatened to erupt into war. The two sides were the "Slopers" and the "Easterners." Slopers were sporting men from around San Francisco and the mining towns of California and Arizona—the "slopes" of the Sierras. Easterners were gambling men who had pretty well controlled the games in Texas, Colorado, and Kansas. Doc Holliday was an Easterner; so were the Earp brothers.

Until the discovery of silver produced Tombstone, the two sides had mostly kept to their home territories—that is, Arizona wasn't in either area and was of no interest. But the mining bonanza led, as always, to a bonanza for professional gamblers.

Gambling can take place in the sorriest of circumstances, and as firsthand accounts and the few available photos reveal, the early facilities were pretty sorry—tents, jacals, lean-tos, sheds, or tightly jammed ramshackle saloons hastily erected. It was clear that a more-handsome gambling facility would be attractive to the rough miners who, after all, came to town not only to cash out their diggings but to experience at least something more civilized than their crude facilities out at the mines. Of several new properties, the Oriental was the most impressive. It was described in an October 2004 issue of *Wild West* magazine, quoting the *Tombstone Daily Epitaph*:

> *Last evening the portals were thrown open and the public permitted to gaze upon the most elegantly furnished saloon this side of the Golden Gate. Twenty-eight burners suspended in neat chandeliers afforded an illumination of ample brilliancy and the bright rays reflected from the many colored crystals in the bar sparkled like a December icing in the sunshine. The saloon comprises two apartments. To the right of the main entrance is the bar, beautifully carved, finished in white and gilt and capped with a handsomely polished top. In the rear of this stand a brace of side-boards. . . . They were made for the Baldwin Hotel, of San Francisco. . . . The back apartment is covered with a brilliant body brussels [sic] carpet and suitably furnished after the style of a grand club room, with conveniences for the wily dealers in polished ivory . . . Tombstone has taken the lead, and [to] Messrs. Joyce and Co., our congratulations.*

By the time the Oriental opened in July of 1880, the Earp brothers were already in town. Jim was now a bartender in another saloon, Virgil, a deputy US marshal, Morgan, riding shotgun for Wells Fargo, and Wyatt, a deputy sheriff in neighboring Pima County.

The Oriental was owned by Easterners, of course, so it soon faced competition from other saloons in which the Slopers had interests. One of the Slopers, John Tyler, began intimidating customers of the Oriental to drive them away. For "self-protection," Oriental brought in Wyatt Earp as a partner. After sizing up the opposition, Wyatt decided that more strength was called for. He sent for Doc Holliday, Luke Short, and Bat Masterson. Holliday came on the double, Luke Short showed up in September; Bat Masterson would be along early the next year. Some strength!

In October Holliday confronted Tyler in the Oriental. To avoid trouble, Joyce, the bartender, asked them both to leave. Tyler did so. Doc wouldn't, so the bartender, a big hulk of a man, picked up the relatively small Holliday and threw him out. Doc got a gun, came back in, and exchanged shots with Joyce—who then jumped on Holliday and beat him to a pulp. This probably did Doc's reputation no good, but the dance wasn't over yet.

Tyler came back; this time he was jabbing his pistol into the face of the faro dealer. Wyatt Earp was instantly on him, while Doc Holliday held Tyler's henchmen at bay. Wyatt bit into Tyler's ear and threw him out into the street.

The next segment of this war was played out between Short and Charlie Storms. Storms was allegedly a hired gun for the Slopers, and chose to mix it up with Short. It ended with Storms dead and Short, unimpaired. After this the Slopers seem to have gone back into their hole.

About when all this dust had settled Wyatt and his "Easterners" clan picked up another enemy. They were loosely referred to as "the Cowboys" ("rustlers" would have been a bit more accurate). The Earps accused the Cowboy gang of being involved in stagecoach and mail robberies along with their rustling. Bad blood was developing; threats were made. With things heating up, Morgan Earp retrieved Holliday, who had gone to Tucson.

On October 25 two of the Cowboys, Ike Clanton and Tom McLaury, were in Tombstone to buy supplies. That evening Ike, Holliday, and Morgan Earp got into a yelling match with the Cowboys, with Clanton threatening to kill them. Deputy Marshal Virgil Earp stepped in between and threatened to arrest them all. This affair had little to do with poker, but you can't mention Tombstone without saying *something* about the "O.K. Corral" dustup.

Doc and Wyatt went home to sleep, but Virgil, still trying to calm things down, sat down at a poker table with Ike and Tom, plus Sheriff John Behan and an unidentified man. Ike drank all night and stayed pretty drunk. Around daybreak the game broke up, with Ike still mouthing threats against the Earps. Virgil told him he didn't want to hear any more such talk—that he was going home to bed, and Ike had better not cause any trouble.

Alas, Ike and Tom kept on drinking, and Ike retrieved his guns from the West End Corral. At that point Ike was in open defiance of the law against carrying guns in town, *and* he was still loudly mouthing threats against the Earps.

Somebody went to get the Earps. Virgil buffaloed Ike, hammering him with the butt of a six-gun, and arrested him for carrying firearms in the city. (A judge immediately fined Ike $25, which he grousingly paid.)

Then Wyatt buffaloed Tom McLaury for carrying a concealed pistol.

Now two of the Earps had roughed up two of the Cowboys.

After several more Cowboys rode into town, two were seen going into a gun and hardware store. Virgil Earp decided to disarm them, but only if they were still carrying guns in violation of the law. He found them having a confab in a lot near the corral. Virgil decided to enforce the law and disarm them at this point, so he armed himself with pistol and rifle, Doc Holliday tucked

Virgil's shotgun under his long coat, and Virgil, Morgan, Wyatt, and Doc headed down Fremont Street toward the Cowboys.

That's when all hell broke loose. The thirty-second fight ended with three Cowboys dead, and three of the Earp group wounded. Wyatt was unharmed.

The now-legendary "Gunfight at the O.K. Corral" ended nothing. In the following days Tombstone remained in an uproar, with everybody choosing sides; Virgil and Morgan got ambushed, and several more Cowboys were killed.

But poker in Tombstone was alive and well—very alive, as a game in May of 1881 would suggest. At least it began in '81, and lasted until 1889, as described in the following chapter.

CHAPTER THIRTEEN

The Poker Roamers

Beyond Tombstone, beyond Abilene and Wichita and Deadwood and other more-recognizable places, the Old West was full of dedicated poker players.

Poker Alice

Unlike a number of Old West characters, Poker Alice's origin is well-known. She was born Alice Ivers in England of a schoolmaster, which meant that she received more education than usual. While her upbringing was designed to prepare her to become a respected member of Victorian society, her karma had a different idea.

By the time Alice was in her late teens she had become a beauty. She moved with her family to the wilds of Colorado, where she soon married and set up house in Leadville. Her new husband taught her to play poker, and she quickly became a striking presence at the poker tables, as both dealer and player. With the new nickname of Poker Alice, her reputed motto at least referenced her religious childhood: "Praise the Lord and place your bets, I'll take your money with no regrets."

She was quite successful, with poker winnings financing New York shopping trips to purchase the latest Gibson Girl fashions. The high necks, puffy sleeves, and fitted waistlines only added to her charm and hence her popularity as a poker dealer. Sadly, her husband of only a year was killed in a mining accident, leaving Alice to survive alone.

Her poker winnings fortunately sustained her even as, following the excitement of new mining discoveries, she headed for Deadwood, South Dakota. Thanks to her beauty, figure, and charm, she was soon popular among the saloon-keepers and bartenders there.

One day she found herself attracted to a man named Tubbs, who was playing poker at a nearby table. While carefully attending to the game she was dealing, Alice was also glancing frequently at Tubbs. He was doing well—so well that one big fellow angrily pushed his chair back and rose from the table. Tubbs, concentrating on his hand, ignored him.

This large, bearlike man drifted around behind Tubbs. As Tubbs raked in another pot, Alice glimpsed the big man pulling a bowie knife from its sheath. As he drew back the knife, preparing to plunge it into Tubbs's back, Alice calmly shot him. Tubbs waved at her in gratitude; Alice nodded and, smiling, turned her attention back to the hand she was dealing. They were soon married, and eventually had seven children. Alas, Alice again lost her husband, this time to tuberculosis.

When Wild Bill Hickok was killed in Deadwood, Alice raced from the saloon in which she was playing. As she gazed at Hickok's inert body, she said aloud, "Bill had invited me to play this morning, but I was committed to another game. If I'd joined him I would probably have been sitting in that chair he was killed in."

Hearing of new silver strikes, Alice drifted to New Mexico and down to Silver City. Again she was hired to attract gamblers into the spider's web—that is, gambling parlor—a role in which she was again quite successful.

New mining strikes in the West were like magnets, and Alice succumbed to their pull, eventually ending up in the mining town of Sturgis. There, trying to settle a brawl with her rifle, she "accidentally" killed a soldier. Fortunately for Alice, the shooting was ruled an accident.

The hard life of continuously relocating, coupled with late hours and a fair share of alcohol, slowly turned Poker Alice into a fleshy and rotund smoker of big stogies, attired in work shirts and men's hats. Still, Alice kept on playing poker and evidently held no regrets. In her seventies she said, "At my age I suppose I should be knitting, but I would rather play poker with five or six 'experts' than eat."

DICK CLARK

Although he never killed anyone (that we know of), Dick Clark was still one of the leading figures in the Old West poker scene. He was always where the action was hottest, he was a constant winner, and—possibly most surprising—he was scrupulously honest (virtually a defect for an old-time poker player).

The Topeka *Daily Commonwealth* remarked that Clark "had the reputation of being one of the best-hearted and cleverest poker players in the country. His face while engaged in play is one of the most impassive and stony I ever saw."

Clark, born in 1838 in New York, had become a professional gambler by the age of twenty-one, so he was well prepared for infantry barracks and encampment life during the Civil War, where he cleaned out his bunkmates. After the war he followed the action in Abilene, Ellsworth, Newton, Wichita, Dodge City, and, finally, Tombstone.

In Tombstone Clark set up the gambling concession in the Oriental Saloon, and to maintain peace and decorum (!), he hired Bat Masterson, Luke Short, Wyatt Earp, and Doc Holliday. In 1883 he sold out his interest in the Oriental and bought a new business that had risen to become one of the foremost gambling salons of the day: the Alhambra.

At the Alhambra Clark enjoyed hosting and engaging the rich and famous in high-stakes poker games. In a game with Senator

Horace Tabor—whose life was later featured in the opera *The Ballad of Baby Doe*—Clark won a carload of silver ore that was standing on the railroad tracks just out of town. (They *are* different from you and me.)

In the 1880s, Clark ran the famous "longest poker game in history" at the Bird Cage Theatre in Tombstone. It lasted eight years, five months, and three days, nonstop, 24/7/365. The buy-in was $1,000—equivalent to $22,000 today. With no low-rollers involved, participants besides Clark included cattle baron John Chisum, Budweiser founder Adolph Busch, Diamond Jim Brady, George Hearst (mining millionaire, gubernatorial candidate, US senator, and father of William Randolph Hearst), and of course Tombstone stalwarts Doc Holliday, Bat Masterson, and Wyatt Earp.

Think this was just for the fortunate few? The waiting list for the game was four days long. While the game was going on there was also action in the theater upstairs: twenty-six dead from gun and knife fights, leaving 140 bullet holes in ceilings, walls, and floors. But the game went on, until over $10 million had changed hands.

(As strange as it may seem, something similar—minus the bullets—occurs today in places like Las Vegas and Atlantic City. In 2010 poker celebrity Phil Laak played live poker for over 115 hours in the World Series of Poker, seeking to make it into the *Guinness Book of World Records.* The longest *game* was Clark's at the Bird Cage, but Laak may earn the record for the longest continuous game played by one individual. As long as there are willing players, the games go on; the casino does need shifts of dealers, but this is not a problem for the larger ones. It's difficult, though, to imagine how the Bird Cage managed it.)

Clark became a consumption (tuberculosis) patient bent over with alcohol and morphine. In 1888 he married seventeen-year-old Louise d'Argentcourt (well, at least her name *sounded* like royalty), but she didn't restore him, and he died five years later.

By then groundwater seepage from the mines had flooded the Bird Cage Theatre and much of Tombstone. As the mines played out, the population diminished, but the town has continued and is still famous—sort of. It is the home of "The World's Largest Rosebush." In 2014 the bush covered 8,000 square feet, with a trunk that was twelve feet around. So there you are.

BILLY THE KID AND PAT GARRETT

When Wyatt Earp and Doc Holliday hightailed it out of Arizona (with the bloodhounds—actually the sheriff—on their tail), they first landed in Silver City, New Mexico. Silver City is where a young Billy the Kid got his start as a gambler. His start as a killer came later.

Silver City grew up as a mining town named, naturally, for the silver deposits found nearby. It is located on the same site where ancient Mimbres Mogollon Indians once lived. Although archaeologists prize Mimbres pottery, some of which is now in the Smithsonian, locals developed a bad habit of digging up pots and using them for target practice. Laws were passed to forbid such activity, but illegal digging and collecting continues today.

Some of those diggers may be looking for Billy the Kid artifacts instead of pottery. Three law enforcement officials from Lincoln County set out in 2003 to dig up the graves of Billy the Kid in Fort Sumner and his mother, Catherine McCarty, in Silver City. Their aim was to compare the DNA found with such as Brushy Bill and John Miller to prove or disprove their claims to be Billy the Kid. They eventually dug up a grave or two in Arizona and were hit with grave-digging charges (duh!). (They had to resign their Lincoln County Commissions.)

Billy's mother, Catherine McCarty, with her new husband William Antrim and other son Josie, relocated to Silver City in the early 1870s, hoping to cure her tuberculosis. The move didn't work; she soon died, leaving Billy a virtual orphan. (Where was Antrim? Off seeking his fortune in the mines, as usual.)

Shuffled from one home to another, at the age of fourteen Billy not only began to frequent the Orleans Club, where he acquired a fair degree of poker skill, but he also developed a bit of a stealing habit. Nobody seemed to worry about a kid becoming a cardsharp at such a tender age, but stealing was another matter entirely: *That* was against the law. So the sheriff locked him up—not to punish him, but to put him on the straight and narrow.

Billy promptly manifested a characteristic that was present throughout his entire, albeit short, life. He escaped. Using his charm (another constant characteristic), he got the sheriff to let him have the run of the hallway fronting the jail cells during the evening. Billy had noticed a fireplace there, so when the sheriff left for the day, locking the door from the hallway back into his office, Billy contorted himself into the fireplace chimney and wiggled his way up through the soot and out—to freedom.

And away he went, west into Arizona Territory, beyond the reach of the Silver City sheriff, toward Camp Grant. When he got to Arizona Billy was of course quite young, but he was now trying to survive as a man in a man's world, with no mother or dad to guide him. He took any job he could get—first, at a ranch, where he was soon dismissed for being so small and light that he couldn't carry his weight, and then in a cheese plant, followed by jobs cutting hay, driving a wagon, and washing dishes at a restaurant. This was hand-to-mouth survival, and when his new friend John Mackie invited Billy to help him steal some horses, he didn't hesitate. The local sheriff didn't hesitate in arresting him, either; but as was becoming his style, Billy readily escaped custody and slid over to the next camp. The sheriff wasn't going to spend any time chasing an escaped teenaged horse thief.

Billy also found that his youth and innocent look were assets at the card tables in the Atkins Cantina. There was only small change to be earned dealing faro; far better pickings were available playing poker. Along with his winnings Billy was increasing his skill and knowledge at poker, which would stand him in good stead later when he was unable to find a legitimate job.

But poker could also be a source of trouble. One day he and hefty blacksmith Frank Cahill were at the same poker table, and Cahill started "picking on" Billy—something he had done every time they had come together. Billy took it for a while, but when Cahill called him a pimp, Billy responded, "And you're a son of a bitch."

Well, no "real man" was going to stand for *that*. Cahill jumped him and they tussled some, but Cahill was considerably larger, or just fatter, so he was able to get Billy down on the floor, where he proceeded to whale the tar out of him. Billy protested, "Stop it! You're hurting me." Cahill laughed, "What do you think I mean to do, boy?"

Now the cowboy way, or the code of the West, or the rules of machismo—somewhere in the psyche of men in the Old West— demand that you not take that kind of beating. Billy worked his pistol out from under his side, poked the muzzle against Cahill's big belly, and let fly.

Cahill died. Billy was arrested and jailed to wait for the grand jury. Nobody knew how long that would be, so Billy did what by now was becoming his shtick—he slipped away.

Adios, Arizona. Time to retry old Mexico. According to Pat Garrett's *The Authentic Life of Billy the Kid*, he first heard Sonora calling. Remember, by this time Billy was still truly a kid, maybe sixteen, so it was hard to get respected at the poker table. But respect gradually came with winning.

One dealer would single Billy out for razzing. This dealer kept his pistol on the table. Finally Billy asked him if he would fight as bravely with his pistol as he did with his mouth. Again, the code of the West ruled: The dealer grabs for his pistol, but Billy is faster and kills him. He goes off to Chihuahua, where a similar story plays out: The kid does well in poker, which antagonizes the dealer, who claims he doesn't have enough pesos to pay Billy his winnings. Strangely enough, that night the dealer was robbed. Apparently, things could have been worse; after another dealer called Billy a little runt, the man disappeared, never to be heard from again.

These tales *may* have happened—in *The Authentic Life of Billy the Kid* Pat Garrett says they did. But they may not have. No other writer has, to my knowledge, ever confirmed Garrett's stories. Now it's not my place to call the man a liar, so I'll just move on.

Back in New Mexico Billy fell in with John Kinney's outlaw gang for at least one horse raid, then made his way to Mesilla. There he won some bucks at poker in the Lapoint Saloon. With that grubstake he was ready to head out, but the pony he stole belonged to the sheriff's daughter. Shucks. Better vamoose, pronto.

Billy worked his way over to the Pecos River and got hired as a cowboy by John Tunstall. Tunstall, a young British investor, had angered Jimmy Dolan, the Santa Fe Ring's man in Lincoln and owner of the main store. Tunstall figured he could offer better prices than Dolan so he opened a competing store in Lincoln. Dolan didn't tolerate competition; he had Tunstall killed. This enraged the Tunstall employees and their compadres; they formed a troupe, called themselves the Regulators, and went after the killers. In return a group called Dolan's Boys went after the Regulators, and the Lincoln County War was on. President Hayes now called the road through Lincoln "the most dangerous street in America."

Billy and the other Regulators killed some, lost some, and in the end, lost the war. There were still too many killings and murderous threats in Lincoln County, so the new governor, Lew Wallace, issued a blanket amnesty to get the men back to their farms and ranches. It applied to everyone in the Lincoln County War—except Billy the Kid, meaning he alone was outlawed. And the new sheriff, Pat Garrett, was after him.

But Billy could still gamble. Even outside of Lincoln, there were saloons and card games in places like Las Vegas, White Oaks,

San Patricio, and Puerto de Luna. So cards and some cattle rustling kept Billy going.

Las Vegas was a hotbed of gamblers and gunfighters. One night Billy was even honored to have dinner with Jesse James—although he turned down Jesse's invitation to join forces and go rob some trains. Las Vegas was fun, but there were newspapers and telegraphs, trains and stagecoaches—too much intercourse for a wanted outlaw to hang around too long, so both Billy and Jesse hit the road, but in opposite directions.

Then there was Fort Sumner, a favorite because it had Miss Paulita Maxwell and other charming señoritas with whom to dance, and Beaver Smith's Saloon for good, loose poker games. In a letter Billy sent to Governor Wallace pleading for amnesty, he (unwisely) wrote, "I have been in Sumner since I left Lincoln, making my living gambling."

Unfortunately, Billy became overconfident in his hopes for amnesty. Garrett and some of his posse had gone to Fort Sumner after hearing that Billy was camped nearby. They hid out in the old fort hospital building, and one evening were playing poker on a blanket spread on the floor when Billy and several pals boldly rode up. Garrett and his men let fly a hail of bullets, wounding compadre Tom O'Folliard, but Billy and the others escaped untouched.

The lawmen dragged O'Folliard into the room and laid him on the floor, where he moaned over his pain. One of the posse said, "Shut up and take your medicine," and the men resumed their poker game. (In the Old West, poker sometimes took precedence over anything else.) O'Folliard soon died.

The next day the posse began scouring the area and caught up with Billy and the others at a place called Stinking Springs, east of Fort Sumner. Billy was captured, tried, convicted, and sentenced to hang. Well, you know Billy—he escaped.

A bit later he sneaked back into Fort Sumner—whether for love or just chutzpah is not clear. This time Garrett was hiding in Pete Maxwell's room; as Billy entered, Garrett shot and killed him.

Deluvina Maxwell was a Navajo woman Lucien Maxwell had bought from the Apaches; she had taken the Maxwell name. Deluvina was very fond of Billy. On one visit to Fort Sumner he won a large sum of money in a poker game and asked Deluvina to sew the money into the seam of a new pair of pants. She did, and he was wearing those pants when he was killed. She said the pants and money were buried with him. (When Deluvina saw that Garrett had killed Billy, she began beating his chest, declaring, "You pees-pot. You son of a bitch. You have killed my Billito!")

Killing Billy didn't make Pat Garrett rich, but it did make him famous. This was a man who, until that moment, had done nothing to get his name in the history books. Like many men in the Old West, he had knocked around doing a number of things: hunting buffalo, raising pigs, bartending, and even peddling stolen cattle to the butchers in Las Vegas.

But, he also loved to gamble. Before he became sheriff, Pat and Billy certainly knew each other, probably faced off over the poker table, and may or may not have been friends; historians debate it. At least Pat knew of Billy's love for poker and his attachment to Fort Sumner. In the end that was the key to catching him.

After killing Billy, Garrett bounced around—as a Texas Ranger for a short while, as sheriff in New Mexico's Dona Ana County, and as collector of customs in El Paso. For the latter job he was interviewed by President Theodore Roosevelt, who noted that he had heard Garrett was a gambler. Pat replied, "I know the difference between a straight and a flush, Mr. President, and in my section of the country, a man who doesn't know this doesn't know enough to keep the flies off." Since Teddy Roosevelt was known to like poker himself, Garrett got the appointment. But it was rocky, and he was soon canned.

Then in 1908 Garrett got into a dispute with a man named Rhode over a lease. As they were riding along and arguing Garrett stopped and walked behind a tree to relieve himself. Rhode summarily blew him away with a bullet in the back.

The cattleman John Chisum's wife Sallie knew both Billy the Kid and Pat Garrett. She said that "there was good mixed with the bad in Billy the Kid and bad mixed with the good in Pat Garrett. But both were real men, and worth knowing."

BELLE STARR

In the Old West a studly guy might be called a "real man." Oklahoma's Belle Starr, "The Best Lady Gambler in the West," wasn't a real man—but she was surely a real woman. Not someone you'd want to challenge face-to-face. As she famously said, "A pair of six-shooters beats a pair of sixes anytime."

Belle Starr started out, in 1848, as Myra Maybelle Shirley. Born in Missouri to a reasonably wealthy family, she attended Carthage Female Academy. Her strong personality quickly rose to the fore; a classmate remembered her as "a bright, intelligent girl but of a fierce nature who would fight anyone, boy or girl, that she quarreled with." As a child she was at least energetic, old-timers might even say rambunctious. She sang, she danced, she played the piano—not only at home but in a local inn, which is where she received some very helpful lessons in card playing.

After she became famous, Belle was described as beauteous, voluptuous, gorgeous, lovely—but also as "bony and flat chested with a mean mouth; hatchet faced; gotch-toothed tart." Pictures I've seen show a rather attractive younger woman (but never as attractive as the stars who portrayed her in movies) who did not age gracefully.

Belle customarily wore two revolvers, high-topped boots, and a Stetson hat with an ostrich plume to complement her tight black jacket, chiffon waists, and velvet skirts. And she mostly rode sidesaddle, considered more ladylike. Like Belle Siddons, Belle Starr spied for the Confederacy's Quantrill Raiders during the Civil War. Although arrested by Yankees and held as a spy, she was soon released. Afterward the family moved to Texas, just outside Dallas.

By this time Belle, it is said, was an expert at poker and faro. She spent most of her time in Dallas playing cards; her gambling skills became sharper than ever, and she was a regular winner. Belle actually helped support her family from poker winnings and as a faro dealer. That was how she met Jim Reed, a veteran Confederate soldier turned outlaw. It was love at first sight, and they were soon married. Jim would go out "with the boys" on raids and Belle would stay at the card table, where she not only made money but also picked up useful information about gold and payroll shipments, which she would then pass on to Jim.

Sad to say, Jim got himself killed. By this time Belle had experienced a taste of the risk and thrill of banditry, so she took Jim's place in the gang. She also taught the boys the finer points of faro and five-card draw; they were so impressed that some called her the "best lady gambler in the West."

The band would hook up with outlaws in the untamed Indian Territory, including the Youngers and the James gang. During the next few years Belle lived off and on with other outlaws, including Bluford Duck, known generally as Blue Duck.

Blue Duck had apparently not yet been schooled by Belle in poker. He borrowed the gang's money, went into Dodge City, and lost it in a crooked poker game ("crooked" is sort of redundant, but not totally).

Belle took this as a personal insult—"You mess with my family, you're messing with me." She marched into the saloon where the game was going on. Blue had described the other players, and she found them still at the table. The man she was after was tall, had a silver beard and mustache, and was impeccably attired, with an enormous diamond stickpin fronting his cravat. Belle stood behind him a moment, reached down and touched the diamond, and asked, "Did you buy this shiny rock with the money you've stolen from honest gamblers?"

The gambler swatted her hand away, angrily declaring, "This game is closed, and even if it wasn't it's by invitation only. Get the hell out of here."

Belle smiled gently, pulled one of her pistols out of her pocket, and laid it up alongside the tall man's face. "Not time for me to leave just yet. You cheated a friend of mine out of $2,000 a little while ago. I'm here to take it back." The pistol didn't move.

The gambler now spoke more meekly. "You know you can land in the Bastille for this kind of behavior."

"Then why don't you call the sheriff," Belle growled. "He might be interested in your style of playing too."

By this time the other players at the table, who had been sitting there quietly, began to drift away. "You boys go ahead," Belle said. "My beef is only with this long drink of water." Then she reached down and gathered up the pot, which held over $3,000. "This is a little more than I came for, but I'll just keep it all as compensation for my trouble." She backed slowly away, her eyes glued on those of the tall gambler. He didn't move. Belle smiled as she felt the swinging doors behind her, and disappeared.

She returned the $2,000 to Blue Duck, but first made him listen to her lecture on evils—not of poker, but of playing against professional swindlers without first having schooled himself in recognizing the signs of cheating.

Not only was Belle well-educated—the other gang members couldn't read or write—but she was also more imaginative when it came to planning their "engagements." Even though they were a cantankerous bunch, they accepted her leadership. She actually cussed out Cole Younger, saying "I'm not about to become a kitchen slave for you and this outfit of punks."

With Belle doing the planning and more or less in charge, the gang's horse-stealing ventures went more smoothly. They usually got away without arousing an outcry, and by the time the law came looking for them, the contraband beasts had been disposed of profitably. She became known as the Queen of Desperados.

In 1882 Belle and outlaw Sam Starr were arrested (they may have been married by this time). Taken before Fort Smith's "Hanging Judge" Isaac Parker, they were found guilty and sentenced to jail: Belle for six months and Sam for a year.

Soon after his release, Sam died in a shoot-out. Belle was ambushed some time later, killed by a shotgun blast in the back. She was forty-one years old. They never found the murderer, although speculation held that it was her son. Belle Starr was buried clasping the pearl-handled pistol that had been given to her by Cole Younger.

JOHN WESLEY HARDIN

Down in Texas, John Wesley Hardin didn't mimic Belle Starr's life of banditry, but in another way he was no less violent. He killed more men than Billy the Kid—even more than Billy claimed.

What we know about the life of John Wesley Hardin, who was born in central Texas in 1853, comes mainly from his own autobiography, *The Life of John Wesley Hardin, As Written by Himself*. Wes Hardin, as he was usually called, was an inveterate poker player. Even more so than was the case for other famous gunslingers in the Old West, poker and gambling were Hardin's main job, his career. He was not a lawman, nor was he an outlaw in the more traditional sense of one who robbed stagecoaches and banks. He may have stolen a few head of cattle, like most men in the Old West, but he didn't make his living as a rustler.

Of course from our perspective, looking at the whole of Hardin's life, it might be more accurate to say that Wes was simply a killer. He killed freely, at will, for the slightest insult or provocation. But he didn't kill to rob or steal. Therefore, in his eyes, and indeed, in his own words, his killings were all justified and thus righteous.

Hardin killed his first man at the age of fifteen. He said the man "tried to bully" him. Poker wasn't involved—yet. But as a kid, Wes played poker "whenever I got the chance."

Early on he grew to be a near-obsessive gambler. When only sixteen he got into a poker game with a couple of fellows named Bradley and Davis. Hardin believed Bradley, Davis, and a local judge were aiming to fleece him. By midnight he had won all the money on the table, but a disagreement developed over how much Bradley owed Wes. Bradley cussed him out, then drew a big knife and charged. Hardin's partner got between them, giving Wes a chance to bust through a window and head for his boardinghouse. There he grabbed a gun, intending to go back and confront Bradley.

But Bradley and a gang met him as he came out the door. Bradley started blasting away. Although Hardin was still a kid, he coolly turned and fired two shots; the first hit Bradley in the heart, the second, in the head. The gang wisely ran.

For all the fights and shootings, there was one pregnant occasion that could easily have ended in gunshots, but didn't. As Hardin recounted in his autobiography, he was in a game with famed gunfighter Bill Longley. Hardin had four jacks at the showdown. Longley said, "Reckon I've got you, son," and turned over a full house. Hardin replied, "Hold on, I have two pair." Longley: "They are not worth a damn." Turning over his cards, Hardin said, "I reckon two pair of jacks are good," and ended the game ahead $300.

(As noted earlier with George Devol, this "slow-play" act would get him chewed out or worse in poker today. So I doubt that it happened this way, especially against a gunslinger like Longley; Hardin was probably jazzing it up for his autobiography.)

Then there was one evening when, after winning well at poker, Wes had hooked up with a local girl. He was just "getting comfortable" with her when in charged her boyfriend, demanding a hundred dollars.

Sounds like a standard setup, doesn't it? But there was one solution for Wes. It seems there was *always* one solution for Wes. First he pretended to be shaking with terror and started rummaging through his pants for money, "accidentally" dropping a gold coin on the floor. The boyfriend snatched it off the floor and came up looking into the muzzle of Hardin's pistol. Hardin then shot him between the eyes. That was his eighth killing, and he was still only sixteen.

Somehow or other, Hardin survived to the age of eighteen, at which time he got on as a working cowboy with a cattle drive going up the Chisholm Trail. Hardin was excited when the herd reached Abilene, Kansas. For a young man who loved poker and was fond of action, not excluding guns, Abilene by 1871 must have seemed like an Old West Gay Paree. Now he could dress like he thought a real, professional gambler would dress: conservative suit and vest, with no "bling" or flash except for the customary pinkie ring.

In Abilene he undoubtedly had Wild Bill Hickok on his mind. Hickok was town marshal and already had an impressive "rep," especially among aspiring gunsels. Possibly Hardin hoped to build his own reputation by getting into a gunfight with Wild Bill.

But it didn't work out like that.

Ben Thompson was already in Abilene, and Ben Thompson also had an impressive rep—as a bad egg and troublemaker. His brother Jim was constantly having to bail him out, getting him out of a problem Ben himself had stirred up. In this case, Ben had entered a partnership with Phil Coe in the Bull's Head saloon. Marshal Hickok had told them to change their crude sign that featured an explicit and overly endowed bull; they didn't, so he painted over it. Coe felt that Hickok's action was humiliating, and stewed about how to get even.

Loyal partner Thompson decided to find someone to "get" Wild Bill. Hardin, the young newcomer and alleged gunfighting hotshot, just come to town, ought to be about right.

Thompson started telling Hardin bad things about Hickok— how he was a Yankee and always picked out Southern men to kill, especially Texans. But Wes just told Thompson that he didn't do anyone else's fighting, only his own, and that if he needed Hickok killed he could go do it himself. Ben Thompson may have been a troublemaker, but he was no hero. He backed off.

Instead of looking for Hickok, Hardin went looking for a poker game. Didn't take much looking in Abilene, of course. After a drink in a barroom on the plaza, he found a game in the back room. According to Wes, he won the pot and invited the others to the bar, then after a drink headed out to the street, where he immediately ran into Hickok.

Hardin was wearing two guns. Bill told him to take the guns off—that he was under arrest. As described in the Hickok section, Hardin claims he pulled both guns out, but as Hickok was reaching for them Hardin did a road agent's spin, whirling them over so the muzzles were in Bill's face. Hickok just shrugged and walked on.

Most historians doubt that this ever happened. In his book on Hardin, Leon Metz concluded (after somewhat tortuous reasoning) that it probably did happen because it was a way for Hardin to demonstrate his mastery of Wild Bill Hickok without risking his life.

But something like the incident could very well have occurred, because Hardin's trail boss had already "posted" him to Hickok. This was common practice with Chisholm Trail herds. On arrival, the foreman would pay the sheriff or marshal a bribe to go easy on his men, and not throw them in the hoosegow for a little rambunctiousness. Further, he would promise to stand good for any fine that might be levied against one of his cowboys.

At any rate, noted gunslinger John Wesley Hardin and famed gunfighter Wild Bill Hickok became loose friends and played poker together in Abilene, one night winning over $1,000 apiece ($19,000 each in today's dollars).

After one hard evening playing poker, Hardin took a room in the American House Hotel. He needed sleep. Too bad; pal Charles Couger was in the next room, and he turned out to be a stentorian snorer. Hardin banged on the wall, to no avail. Now irritated, he sent several shots through the wall. He later claimed he aimed high, just to silence Couger, but one shot was obviously low enough to kill his pal.

Hardin climbed out the second-story window, leapt to the ground, and spotted Hickok coming. He took off, burrowed his way into a haystack, hid out the rest of the night, stole a horse, and headed for his cow camp. He left the next day for Texas.

Back in Texas, and indeed wherever he went, Hardin continued to practice two specialties: poker and killing. In his autobiography, he claims ten gunfights and eleven killings from 1871 to 1876. In 1876 he was arrested in Mobile, Alabama, for using marked cards. He got away. While on the run, two formerly enslaved people tried to apprehend him and he shot them, killing one and blinding the other.

Texas governor Richard Hubbard finally got fed up and put out a $4,000 reward ($76,000 today) for Hardin. It took a couple of years, but Texas Rangers along with local lawmen caught Hardin on a train in Florida. He tried to draw on them but his pistol got caught in his suspenders (now that's humiliating). The Rangers knocked him unconscious. He was tried, convicted, and sentenced to twenty-five years in Texas's Huntsville Prison.

In prison Hardin tried several times to escape, unsuccessfully. He tried to steal guns from the prison armory, again unsuccessfully. His wife Jane died. He apparently gave up and turned, at least while in prison, to more peaceful behavior. He read theological books, became superintendent of the Sunday School, and studied law. It's not reported, but if the jailers allowed it you can be sure he played poker—and winning would have been relatively easy.

In 1894, while still a young man of forty, Hardin was released from Huntsville. He had served seventeen years. His lawyer got Governor Hogg to issue a pardon, then Hardin passed the bar exam and was licensed to practice law.

Wes married a fifteen-year-old child named Callie Lewis, but the marriage soon ended (although they never formally divorced). One story is that Wes won Callie from her father in a poker game.

In El Paso Hardin practiced law, played poker, and drank. His law business was minimal, and his poker-playing skills had mostly left him (sometimes after a loss he would just grab the pot and dare anyone to challenge him). He drank a lot.

Biographer Metz tried to figure out how much Hardin drank from his bar bills. Metz's calculations show that it worked out to the equivalent of thirty beers or twenty whiskey shots a day.

Hardin's mistress, "the widow M'Rose" (not Callie Lewis) was arrested by El Paso policeman John Selman Jr., the son of John Selman. An angry Hardin challenged young John and then pistol-whipped him. Papa John heard all this and stepped in, which resulted in a fierce argument between him and Hardin. But no gunplay.

The younger Selman had headed a gang called Selman's Scouts that marauded in Lincoln County, New Mexico Territory, following the Lincoln County War. They were full-service outlaws who rustled horses and cattle, robbed and ransacked villages and homes, raped women, and murdered men and boys. Governor Lew Wallace finally threatened martial law. So Selman decamped to El Paso, where he worked as a constable to supplement his gambling.

After the face-off with John senior, Hardin repaired to the Acme Saloon. Selman Jr. came in and the two played cards off and on. Around eleven o'clock, Selman went outside and sat sulking on a barrel, evidently brooding about Hardin. Soon he was back in the Acme, where Hardin was now rolling dice for drinks with a man named Brown.

Hardin had just rolled and said, "Okay, Brown, you have four sixes to beat," when Selman shot Wes in the back of the head, plus three more times after he fell. Selman was arrested and, of course, got off by claiming Hardin was going for a gun. The jury promptly acquitted him on grounds of self-defense. (Don't know why "four sixes" didn't become known as the "dead man's hand.")

And that's just the way it was, in the Old West—at least in El Paso.

CHAPTER FOURTEEN

Poker in the New West

As we've seen, in the Old West poker virtually dominated life. Steamboaters, miners, trappers, Indians, gunfighters, lawmen, cowboys, soldiers, bandits, prostitutes—all seemed to spend their leisure time playing poker and related card games like faro and monte. For many, poker was simply their raison d'être, even if their reputations and fame were fed by other actions.

But with the back-to-back devastating droughts and blizzards of 1886–1887, the Old West, as generally perceived in popular culture, was gone. Three-fourths of the cattle had died in the blizzards, the ranges were fenced, and cattle drives weren't much needed because trains ran everywhere. Steamboats had been replaced by rail, which was less leisurely and offered fewer opportunities for sharpsters like George Devol to spend days developing trust and then milking passengers. Beaver in the Rockies had been mostly trapped out. The fantastic mine discoveries had been discovered and developed; smaller deposits still existed, but they no longer provided the stuff of legends.

The cowboy era ended. The open range was fenced in, and major cattle drives became a thing of the past. Indians had been imprisoned on reservations; cowboys and Indians no longer fought.

Yes, the times they were a-changin'.

How would the poker players of the Old West fare in today's games, and particularly in the World Series of Poker? I can imagine a final table where out of the thousands of entrants the final survivors are Wyatt Earp, Lottie Deno, Wild Bill Hickok, Doc Holliday, Poker Alice, John Wesley Hardin, Bat Masterson, Calamity Jane, and Luke Short. In the midst of a lot of good-natured banter, Poker Alice would growl "Shuffle up and deal!"

As the nineteenth century came to an end, the twentieth brought us Teddy Roosevelt with his "big stick" and charge up San Juan Hill, the first war to end all wars, the Roaring Twenties and the Great Depression, and then the next war to end all wars. Poker continued, but laws in most states meant that it had to be kept out of sight, under the table.

That didn't stop our presidents from playing.

POKER IN THE WEST WING

Poker has continued to be supported by a string of poker-playing presidents. Even George Washington liked to play cards, though probably not any version of poker, since it wasn't really developed until up in the nineteenth century. And despite his own fondness for cards, during the Revolutionary War Washington decided that card playing was detrimental to good order and morale, so he forbade it.

Ulysses S. Grant was one of the first presidents to embrace poker. Grant certainly knew about the game from his days in the Civil War, and either used poker to improve his assessment of General Sheridan's character, or used his knowledge of Sheridan to beat him at the table. For example: One night in a game including the two of them, Grant took three cards on the draw and Sheridan stood pat—said he'd play with the five he'd been dealt. Sheridan then bet the max and Grant, after looking Sheridan over while chomping on the black stub of a cigar, raised the limit. Sheridan reraised and so did Grant—the pot was getting huge.

Finally Sheridan stood pat and merely called Grant's last raise. Grant turned over a pair of nines with a big grin; Sheridan had nothing. Laughing, Grant said, "I knew you were bluffing,

Phil, and I would have kept raising you until my whole pile was in the pot."

Helps to know your opponent.

Even before President Grant, Kentuckian and would-be president Henry Clay was not only a great orator but also a pretty good poker player. Once in an exclusive Southern club, a stranger sat down at Clay's table and was soon involved in the biggest pot of the evening. At the showdown the stranger turned over three aces and reached for the pot.

Clay told him to "jist hold on a minute." He got up and went over to the wall where his giant bowie knife was hanging in its sheath. He pulled out the knife, ambled back to the table, and using the point, flipped over his own hand: two pairs: tens . . . and aces. Poker decks just don't come with *five* aces.

The stranger mumbled something about needing to go and dashed for the door, of course leaving the pot untouched. Clay wheeled around after him, drawing back his arm to throw the knife. Just then another player yelled, "Stick him in the ace!" Clay roared with laughter, which convulsed his arm, and the knife landed in the doorjamb.

Ol' Henry might have made a very interesting president.

Like any good president, Grover Cleveland was always watching and listening to learn more about his Cabinet members and other associates. One device he used was poker. You can learn a lot about people through several hands at the poker table—are they risky or cautious, garrulous or closemouthed, generally believable or chronic liars, aggressive or passive? Do they hoard money or use it as a tool?

Once, near the end of Cleveland's term, he played against House Speaker Carlisle, Navy Secretary Whitney, Senator Cameron of Pennsylvania, and a Southern politician named Patterson. Patterson was dealt a pat flush (that is, five cards of one suit on the first deal). The president got a pat full house (beats a flush). Cameron and Patterson bet the maximum, Carlisle called, Cleveland quietly called; he was more than willing for the others to build the pot. Cameron drew one card, the president and Patterson stood pat, and poor Carlisle drew four cards to go with the singleton he had retained.

At the showdown, Carlisle turned over four kings—to the shock of all the others.

"Take the money, Carlisle, take the money," said the president. "If I'm ever president again I'll make you my secretary of the treasury. But don't you make that four-card draw too often." Cleveland did become president again—and Carlisle was his secretary of the treasury. (Personally, I would be concerned about appointing a man as secretary of the treasury who had called a maximum opening bet with nothing but a high card.)

Although Teddy Roosevelt entered the White House with the assassination of President McKinley, he got his start in politics by socializing and playing poker with Republican bigwigs at party gatherings in a smoky room above a saloon on New York's East Fifty-ninth Street (not unlike Barack Obama—see page 147). Roosevelt later used poker phrasing to explain his proposed "Square Deal": "When I say I believe in a square deal I do not mean to give every man the best hand. All I mean is that there should not be any crookedness in the dealing."

Then there was Warren G. Harding. He loved booze—and poker. Loved it so much they say he once lost the White House china in a poker match with Louise Cromwell Brooks, Douglas MacArthur's first wife. (Sorry, Mr. Visiting Prime Minister, we now have only paper plates for the state dinner.)

Calvin Coolidge played poker, though not as much as Harding. Herbert Hoover wouldn't allow it in the White House. That never stopped his successor.

Franklin D. Roosevelt loved to play poker, but not for the high stakes of the Old West. He often used poker to assess the character and personalities of new appointees, but he had a firm rule that nobody discuss business during a poker game. FDR thought of himself as a strong player, but those with whom he played said he usually lost more than he won.

His nickel-ante stud games sometimes went on and on. And for the night on which Congress was to adjourn, he had a special game: The moment the Speaker of the House called the White House to tell him Congress was adjourning, the game would end and whoever was ahead at that moment would be declared the night's winner.

On one occasion President Roosevelt was doing badly; Treasury Secretary Morgenthau was way ahead. When the expected call came, Roosevelt took it, hung up without a word, and explained it was someone else—not the Speaker's call. The game thus went on for nearly three more hours, until FDR pulled ahead. *Then*, he had an aide bring him the phone, and he pretended to take a call from the House Speaker announcing adjournment and signaling the game's conclusion.

Wouldn't you know it, the morning papers reported that Congress had adjourned at 9:30 the previous evening, not after midnight. Morgenthau saw the newspaper, went into a rage, and called on Roosevelt to resign. Roosevelt talked him out of it.

FDR's successor, Harry S. Truman, not only liked poker, he was a strong player. He and his comrades in Battery C passed the days in the mud near Verdun during World War I in what they called an "almost continuous poker game," a game that continued later when they were civilians. As a county judge in Independence, Missouri, he hosted weekly games three flights up and across the street from the courthouse. As president he confessed to his wife Bess that he sometimes could hardly wait for the weekend, when they would board the presidential yacht with cronies and play poker as they sailed the Potomac. (They were occasionally joined by a younger Lyndon Johnson, although his interest seemed to lie more in developing political allies for the future than in playing cards.)

Once Winston Churchill was Truman's guest on a train bound for Fulton, Missouri, where the former British prime minister was to give his immediately famous "Iron Curtain" speech. As a poker game started, Churchill was preening himself on his playing prowess. Still, he lost steadily as the game progressed. When he left the car briefly, Truman told the others they needed to ease up on Churchill. The president's military aide, Major General Harry Vaughan, erupted, "But boss, this guy's a *pigeon*." However reluctantly, the guys eased up, but not enough to allow Churchill to go home claiming victory over the Yanks.

Dwight D. Eisenhower began learning poker at the age of eight, his teacher an old bachelor named Davis who lived alone. While the two were fishing together, Davis would lecture a young Ike on probabilities, then grill him on hand percentages in the evenings as they sat around a campfire. Consequently, Ike became a systematic, conservative player who usually won.

Later, when Eisenhower was an army officer, he was in a game that was supposed to be open only to "unmarried men who could afford to lose." One of the players, however, was a young married officer who kept losing until he was backing his play with war bonds his wife had saved up to buy. Eisenhower felt badly about this and conspired with the other players to let the fellow win back his losses. But it turned out not to be so easy. As Ike said, "One of the hardest things known to man is to make a fellow win in poker who plays as if bent on losing every nickel." This experience led Ike to conclude that, at least for himself as a senior military officer, there was too big a danger that losing players would harbor resentment that might last for years, and could impinge on morale throughout the command unit. So Eisenhower switched his interest to bridge.

When a young Jack Kennedy was commanding a PT boat in the South Pacific during World War II, one of his crew tried to teach him poker. But Kennedy showed no interest. Later, as president, Kennedy was evidently involved with weightier matters: the Bay of Pigs, civil rights, Marilyn Monroe.

Lyndon Johnson allegedly played the game well enough to win a sports car from Ronald Reagan—a Chrysler Dual-Ghia, one of only 117 ever made (the story *might* be true). LBJ did play poker enough to freely mix poker analogies into political discussions. For example, regarding the troop buildup in Vietnam, he once told aides, "I think I'm gonna put in my stack in this Vietnamese poker game." (That is, he was going to go "all in," meaning, to bet all his chips.) But he then warned that this could lead to a *long* poker game.

Much more than his predecessors (possibly excepting Truman), Richard Nixon was a poker-playing man. So much so that in the South Pacific during World War II, Ensign Nixon was invited by his commanding officer to join a dinner with Charles Lindbergh. Nixon says he turned him down "because I had a poker game that evening." He later regretted missing the opportunity to meet the national hero.

Nixon claimed he learned stud poker from a fellow naval officer. His style was characteristic of most good players: conservative/tight, quiet, rarely bluffing, aggressive only with a strong hand which would then be played to the max. It helped that he had a terrific memory. He could not only follow what cards had been shown throughout a hand, but could also remember how other players had played, and in what circumstances.

Poker populated much of Nixon's later thinking. For example, after his presidency he said, "Many of the things you do in poker are very useful in politics, and are very useful in foreign affairs. One of the problems you see in foreign affairs, especially dealing with great leaders abroad and particularly those who are adversaries, is the almost insatiable tendency of American politicians to put everything on the table, their inability to know when to bluff, when to call, and, above everything else, to be unpredictable"—or as Kenny Rogers sang in "The Gambler," "Know when to walk away."

In one six-handed game Nixon didn't play as tightly as he should have. It was five-card stud; that's one card down and the next four faceup. Usually it's played with betting after each card, but in this game all five cards were dealt before the betting began. Nixon had received the jack, king, ten, and queen of diamonds up—and the ace of diamonds facedown: a royal flush (odds against being dealt one are 649,739 to 1).

The first to bet had a pair showing; he opened with $5. Next player raised to $10. Now it's Nixon's bet, with three players to follow. Experienced players would have quietly called the $10, with the possibility that another player or two would raise and, when the betting came around, the opener or first raiser might raise again. This could continue, depending on the respective hands, until the pot was quite large. But no, Nixon was so enamored with his hand that instead of quietly calling, he immediately raised the maximum of $10. Since his normally conservative play was well known to the others, everyone promptly folded and Nixon won a measly $15.

But Nixon's worst mistake in the hand was showing his down ace (not required, since everyone else had folded). Better poker players don't show down cards unless someone has called, "Ya gotta pay to see it." Now the other players had confirmed that Nixon wouldn't have raised without a killer hand, whereas if he had raked the small pot and then quietly mucked his hand, they would have been left to wonder.

Some say that Tricky Dick was still thinking about poker strategy when he tried the biggest bluff of his life, on Watergate. Didn't work, because the committee had the tapes.

Possibly still chafing over the loss of his sports car, Ronald Reagan favored golf and horseback riding for relaxation while president. His vice president, and subsequent president, George H. W. Bush, apparently didn't play, although the Morale, Welfare and Recreation Department on the USS *George H. W. Bush* aircraft carrier did stage poker tournaments for the seamen.

Bill Clinton seemed, like Kennedy, to be overburdened with other issues—Mogadishu, Somalia, Waco, NAFTA, Bosnia/Serbia—as well as Gennifer Flowers, Paula Jones, Monica

Lewinsky, and so on. After he left office, however, he did have time to show up at the Clinton Foundation Charity Poker Event, although he apparently never took a hand.

If George W. Bush played any poker as president, the stories were kept quiet—although there are tales of poker during his fraternity days at Yale. No, George W. is noted (unfortunately, in the eyes of Internet players) for signing the Unlawful Internet Gambling Enforcement Act banning online poker. (I enjoyed a lot of Internet poker before it became illegal in most of the United States. It was nice to sign on after dinner and relax for an hour or so in a small tournament—and they were pretty easy to beat then. You can find sites on which to play online now, but it's more difficult.)

Barack Obama may have played poker recreationally while in office, but the significance of poker in his political life lies in the games he played with fellow state senators in Illinois, in which the networking served him well in later races and in office.

I don't know whether Donald Trump plays much poker, but the US Poker Championship was held at Atlantic City's Trump Taj Mahal for fifteen years.

So most presidents played poker. That's not particularly surprising; so did most Americans (don't you?), although probably not as much as in the days of the Old West. There's a saying that, until the age of eighteen, baseball is America's pastime, and after that, it's poker.

DRIVEN UNDERGROUND
There was a period, though, when poker was virtually driven underground.

When the troops came home at the end of World War II, the poker that had kept them from going insane in foxholes and tents and ships, under sometimes constant, horrible fire, was now not so acceptable to a society bitten by the Puritan bug. Poker continued to be played, but not as publicly anymore.

With the game mostly out of sight, it is not surprising that "nonplaying" members of society began to look down their noses at any mention of poker—like it was sort of close to pornography. If you played, you generally kept quiet about it, and for sure you didn't brag.

Of course poker, and any other card game with money stakes, was technically illegal in most states. The gambling ban extended to games like golf and betting on baseball, basketball, football, and such. But people kept on gambling, at bridge, golf, horse races, the stock market. So the intolerance for gambling was often manifested by persons who themselves participated regularly in gambling.

During this period when poker was mostly socially unacceptable, some tough fellows down in Texas found this environment to be just to their liking. From the end of World War II into the 1970s, their kingpin was a pudgy-looking, kindly-seeming fellow who wore a big cowboy hat (although he looked most uncowboyish) named Benny Binion.

CHAPTER FIFTEEN

Benny Binion

Trust everyone, but always cut the cards.

—Benny Binion

Benny Binion was born in 1904 just north of Dallas, but at an early age he happily left the farming life for the bright lights of the city. With no education to speak of, he gravitated toward low-level crime in Dallas, getting mixed up in back-alley craps games, penny-ante poker, and thievery. He soon "matriculated" into bootlegging—heck, *every*body was doing it in Dallas—then added the numbers racket, essentially a lottery that could be easily manipulated.

Benny was always ambitious, and he kept reaching for new territory for both of his new "enterprises." Soon enough he was getting messages from established mobsters to stop trying to encroach on their territories. Being young and brash, he often responded with a shotgun. Or occasionally, a baseball bat. Sometimes a homemade bomb. They worked. His businesses continued to expand.

The authorities were another matter. A shotgun might not be the best response, but envelopes of cash did the job just as well. One killing was a little too obvious and he was indicted for murder. They had the evidence, so Binion pleaded guilty. But then he got off with a suspended sentence! How could that happen? Later comments from Binion's son Ted suggested that Benny was willing to plead guilty because he already had a deal in place. (More envelopes, perhaps?)

Benny Binion was developing a "rep" in Dallas. He opened or bought into several illegal casinos, including the elegant Top o' the Hill outside of Fort Worth (in little Arlington, where the police were cheaper). His regular customers included H. L. Hunt, Clint Murchison, and Howard Hughes, and six-figure stakes were common. (Hunt was, of course, the Texas oil tycoon who obtained title to much of the East Texas Oil Field, with one of the world's largest oil deposits; Murchison was another oil nabob and eventually owned the Dallas Cowboys; Hughes was a big shot in the Hollywood film industry, owner of Hughes Aircraft and then Trans-World Airlines, and a world-class weirdo.)

Over some twenty years Benny Binion rose to become the undisputed crime boss of Dallas in another Texas success story—unschooled poor kid works hard and makes good. Good enough, in fact, that the Mafia approached him with a partnership deal. He turned it down. It was a dangerous decision, but when their hit men came to town, the sheriff, well-bought by Benny, plus a crew of his deputies met them at the train station and persuaded them to return the way they had come.

Benny still had local competitors, of course. One of them, Herbert Noble, lost his wife to a car bomb. Noble figured the bomb was meant for him and that Benny Binion was behind it. So he installed bomb racks on a plane, loaded them with improvised explosive devices—homemade bombs—and took off for Benny's home. But the state police headed him off. Noble later lost his head to a pipe bomb in his mailbox, planted, of course, by parties unknown.

In those days the cops and politicians had to get their cut. That was just a normal cost of business to Binion until, as he phrased it, "My sheriff got beat in the election." His control over the police and politicians of Dallas was waning and, "what the hell," Prohibition had been repealed anyway and bootlegging was no longer profitable.

So Benny loaded a wad of cash, his wife, and five kids into his Cadillac and headed for Vegas. There he took over the old El Dorado, renaming it Binion's Horseshoe Club (later, the Golden Horseshoe). No more the old, violent Benny. Oh well, maybe some of it. For example, he generally didn't bother law enforcement in Vegas with suspected cheats or security problems; he just had his thugs beat the crap out of them. Occasionally they didn't get up.

But he still had relations with the cops—again, through fat envelopes. And he offered much more of the same for senators, judges, prosecutors, mayors, and anybody else who could help Benny if he kept them happy and hurt him if he didn't. Being free with large sums was just a cost of doing business, like the occasional fine.

At some point between 1949 and 1951, Binion arranged "the biggest game in town" in Las Vegas. It was a heads-up, no-limit, winner-take-all poker marathon between two of the best poker players he knew, to be played near the front of his casino in full public view. The game featured Nick "the Greek" Dandolos, who held a degree in philosophy, against Johnny Moss, a Texas road gambler whose formal education ended at the second grade. During a break in the game Dandolos chaperoned Albert Einstein along Las Vegas's Fremont Street, introducing him as "Little Al from Pittsburgh—he controls lotta the action 'round Jersey." The game lasted five months, with sleep breaks every four or five days, and finally ended when Dandolos stood, saying, "Mr. Moss, I have to let you go," and reached to shake Moss's hand. Moss had won the marathon.

All that may be true. Or some of it. Or . . .

For all the stories of mobsters, beatings, killings, and bribes, one part of Benny Binion's reputation stood him in good stead in running a casino, and particularly its poker games: His games were scrupulously honest. As journalist Andy Bellin said, "He was known for being an honest criminal." When you sat down at a poker table in the Golden Horseshoe, you might get beat by the run of cards or the skill of the other players, but not by a game that the casino had rigged. That makes a big difference to poker players.

In the 1990s I was searching for a game in the DC area. I had heard about one in nearby Arlington, and went alone, unwisely. It was down a dark side street in some kind of mechanical or auto repair shop, closed up but with detritus propped against the walls and throughout the yard. There was an "entrance" around back, down some concrete steps to the bottom, with a doorway you couldn't even see from up above. Inside, a single bare bulb swung over a blanket-covered table. The "welcome" came without smiles or handshakes, and I figured good luck for me would be just getting out of there with my hide, never mind winning a stake.

I survived, and that's why I later welcomed the opportunity to walk into Binion's Horseshoe. It was smoky, crowded, and not elegant, but the word was that the games were honest—not a term you would apply to some of the Texas Road Gamblers.

TEXAS ROAD GAMBLERS

The History Channel says the Texas Road Gamblers "cleaned Texas dry" playing high-stakes poker in the 1950s and '60s. Texas Road Gamblers included Benny Binion, Doyle Brunson, T. J. Cloutier, Johnny Moss, Sailor Roberts, Crandell Addington, and Amarillo Slim. Names to know, games to avoid.

Since poker in Texas was illegal in those days (and remains so today), these men were by definition outlaws. But they were outlaws in the more-colloquial sense as well, existing mostly outside of the world of nine-to-five jobs, normal commerce, and polite society. And like outlaws in the Old West, they carried guns.

Maybe sometimes too many guns. On his website Texas gambler Johnny Hughes tells of a game where you were better off to not be packing:

> Once Ace and Pat Renfro were down near Corpus when some real professional robbers out of Kansas City took down a really big game. They had shotguns and tear gas and the lookout decided to open the door. . . . After they searched every one, they lined them up and announced they were going to search them again and if they found any hidden money, somebody was getting pistol-whipped. Pat Renfro pointed at $300 in his shirt pocket and said, "You missed a little dab." This was long ago and they both said they were pleased to be doing business with real professional robbers because no one got hurt.
>
> The robbers took Ace's Cadillac and promised to leave it down the road with the keys and they were honorable about that. They missed a big paper sack full of Mexican money in the trunk; Ace had been fading craps in Mexico. The laws and the newspaper guy saw Ace counting that Mexican money in the dark and put in the paper the robbers had missed a huge amount, which was not so. At any rate, Ace was robbed at a motel the following night.

T. J. Cloutier was a good baseball, basketball, and football player who played for the University of California in the 1959 Rose Bowl. He has been a major presence at the World Series of Poker (six WSOP bracelets) and the World Poker Tour, and was elected to the Poker Hall of Fame in 2006. But for all that, his most memorable experience is a Texas game he won with *no cards*!

He had been dealt the "nuts"—the best possible hand at that stage of the hand—in a hold 'em game against one other player. In casino poker, the standing rule is that players must protect their cards; this is often accomplished by placing a chip or something like a cigarette lighter on your two face-down cards. Somehow the dealer "raked" Cloutier's cards into the muck, the pile of dead cards in the middle of the table. Cloutier was astounded, but he noticed that his opponent had his head down and hadn't seen Cloutier's cards disappear. So he made a very strong bet, the opponent folded, and Cloutier won with no cards.

(I sat down at a table with T. J. Cloutier once in Atlantic City. But I got up again as soon as I honorably could!)

Doyle Brunson, variously known as "Texas Dolly" and the "Godfather of Poker," was also a basketball star in high school and college, and even drafted into the NBA, but then a knee injury sidetracked him. So he took up illegal poker in the Texas of the 1950s. Brunson recalls having a gun pulled on him several times and being robbed and beaten. Even so, he was acknowledged as a leader of the Texas Road Gamblers. He described the three goals of a Texas gambler in the 1950s and '60s: Find a game, beat the game, and make it to your car without getting shot. "I once went a whole summer without seeing the sun. I would play all night, then sleep all day," he recalled.

Outrunning both the law and the hijackers who preyed on winners of illegal big-money card games, Brunson eventually landed in Las Vegas. There he was one of the early competitors in the World Series of Poker—he's won ten of the championship bracelets, starting in 1976 with the now famous opening hand of 10-2.

In Texas hold 'em the worst possible starting hand is 7-2; you can't even stretch it to a straight. Doyle's hand wasn't far behind, but he stayed in the hand. The card gods smiled on him, and he won the hand and the championship bracelet. The next year—talk about a six-sigma deviation—Brunson did it again, with 10-2. Ever since, that hand has been known as a "Doyle Brunson."

But it's still a crappy opening hand.

Brunson was close friends with another road gambler, Puggy Pearson—which once cost him a bundle. It seems that Puggy was a cheater. He wasn't, like many other players, an occasional cheater. Puggy tried to cheat pretty much all the time. For example, Brunson

once set up a golf match with big-time drug dealer Jimmy Chagra.
Doyle and Puggy were both good golfers, and toward the end of
the game they were $250,000 up.

Doyle, knowing Pearson's reputation, warned him not to cheat.
If anyone was caught cheating, the game would be forfeited. Alas,
Puggy hit one into the rough, and kicked it out; a bodyguard saw
it, the game was forfeited, the money was lost. Brunson was furi-
ous. "What the hell did you do that for?" he sputtered. "We were
way ahead and had the game locked up. And then! Are you nuts?"

Puggy, head down, just mumbled, "I'm sorry, Doyle. I just
couldn't help myself."

Amarillo Slim was, like Doyle Brunson, a Texas Road Gambler whose exploits extended into the twenty-first century. Thomas
Austin Preston Jr.—his real name—was born in 1928 and died
in his eighties, in 2012. Along the way he won a World Series of
Poker, was inducted into the Poker Hall of Fame, and generated
a wagonload of tales and legends, many of which originated with
him.

Slim knew how to cheat, as did most of the better poker players of the day—not so much to win money crookedly as to be
able to spot cheating when in a game, and to protect oneself. For
example, Amarillo Slim was once in a big-money game when he
leaned back in his chair. Not being in the hand, he stretched left
and right, bent at the waist and then leaned his head back—and
spotted a hole in the ceiling. Someone lying up there and peering
through the hole would be able to read Slim's hand, and there was
sure to be a way for that person to communicate with other players
at the table. Slim didn't blow the whistle; he just decided to bide
his time.

Pretty soon the pot was building, until it was quite large;
Slim held his cards so one, a king, was exposed to the watcher
up above. At the showdown, Slim turned his cards over, showing
four aces with a ten. The king had disappeared. The opponent in
the showdown turned red, jumped up, knocking over his chair, but

then froze. He couldn't say a word; anything he might say would give away the fact that he had "somehow" learned about the now-missing king. You don't have to be a cheater yourself to make your knowledge of cheating methods pay off.

Slim loved to bet—he'd bet on anything, "as long as I could get an edge." For example, he beat Minnesota Fats in a pool game in which both had to use a broom for a cue, Evel Knievel in golf with hammers for clubs, and Bobby Riggs in Ping-Pong using frying pans instead of paddles. These all sound unbelievable, until you understand that Slim had, in each case, practiced with the odd device for months before springing the weird bet proposition on his target.

Always a hustler, Amarillo Slim also knew the value of, and how to get, good press. At any poker table, he was the one with the mouth—and probably the only one who could be counted on to give a good quote for the six o'clock news. Plus, he had a "look": big cowboy hat, fancy boots, jewelry, and gold dollars much in evidence. He was in fact a very good poker player, all of which landed him on *The Tonight Show*—not once, but eleven times. Amarillo Slim played against big players and big names: presidents Lyndon Johnson and Richard Nixon, mobsters, and drug lords (Slim was once robbed and left standing in his underwear in a Houston street—until he put in a call to his friend Benny Binion, after which the robbers drove by again and gave him back his money and his trousers). And then there was Willie Nelson—Slim took him for $300,000 in a game of dominoes.

Slim once bet he could outrun the champion racehorse Seabiscuit over one hundred yards—if he could choose the track. He selected a fifty-yard course, which meant both Slim and Seabiscuit would have to do a U-turn at fifty yards and then race back home. In the time it took the jockey to slow the horse and turn around, Slim had sprinted to victory.

Slim also won the World Series of Poker. Of course, with Amarillo Slim you know there's a story here. Slim was a very good poker player—he had to be to survive in the rough environment of the Texas Road Gamblers. But, at least in tournament play, he wasn't as good as some of his Texas pals. Still, Slim always had a strategy, and famously said, "It never hurts for potential opponents to think you're more than a little stupid and can hardly count all the money in your hip pocket, much less hold on to it."

In 1972 the WSOP was in just its third year. A small number of players was soon reduced to three, all Texas Road Gamblers: Puggy Pearson, Doyle Brunson, and Amarillo Slim. Brunson was in the lead with Pearson close behind; Slim was a distant third with the short stack of chips.

Brunson was starting to get worried. Running with the other Texas Road Gamblers, he had been an outlaw most of his life. To protect his wife and three kids he had tried, successfully, to stay out of the spotlight—any big winnings were known only to the other players at the table. And of course he didn't want to attract the attention of the IRS. Brunson was beginning to think that the honor and prestige of winning the WSOP wasn't going to be worth the possible problems with the feds, plus he didn't relish the thought of having a spotlight shining on him and his family nonstop for days following.

Pearson liked the limelight but he didn't really want his dealings made public either. Winning the championship was beginning to look, for him, much like it was looking for Brunson. When the three of them were chatting about the upcoming finish, Brunson and Pearson said they didn't really want to win. Slim popped up, saying, "Well, I do."

This was starting to look like a good solution. They ran it by Jack Binion (Benny's son), who was overseeing the WSOP. Binion was worried that it would look to the public and the media like a fix, so Brunson just decided, "I think I'm getting sick—my stomach's acting up. I'm going home." That left Pearson and Slim. They began to fight it out, fair and square (for the moment, at least). And Slim began to talk. And talk. The media loved it; finally, a poker player who could give good quotes and engage the media in wonderful repartee. Binion began to see the value of Slim becoming the winner.

Slim, a bit out of character, later acknowledged that the final championship was a fix and that he did not actually win the WSOP fair and square. But, the record books say "1972: Amarillo Slim," and that's the way history has recorded it. At any rate, the "managed" outcome gave a tremendous boost to the WSOP's public image, an image that has continued to grow every year.

THE WORLD SERIES OF POKER

It began in 1970. Following a Reno game the preceding year that essentially brought together the best poker players in the country (including Jimmy "The Greek" Snyder, Benny Binion, Doyle Brunson, Amarillo Slim, Johnny Moss, and Puggy Pearson), Binion saw commercial possibilities in doing something similar every year in his Las Vegas Horseshoe Casino.

After several days' play at the Horseshoe with most of the same players, they decided to elect a "world champion." Aw gee, everybody voted for himself. That didn't work. So then they decided to each add a "second best," and *that* person would be crowned. (The first-place vote for yourself couldn't be changed by moving your name to second-best.) This time Johnny Moss emerged as the first world champion, and the World Series of Poker was born.

The game in the WSOP is always the same: Texas hold 'em. It's a game of seven-card stud, except that five of the cards, called "community cards," are dealt faceup in the middle of the table and count as part of every player's hand; two cards are dealt facedown to each individual player. (See appendix A, "Games People Played," for more detail on how the betting proceeds.) Amateurs like it because it looks simple and, with only two cards facedown, they can know most of every hand. Pros like it because, while it looks simple and thus attracts the novices and dilettantes, it is actually a very complex game.

This singular, annual event became a magnet, a focal point for the incredible growth of poker, worldwide, in the succeeding years.

The game stayed in old downtown Vegas at Binion's Horseshoe—crowded, smoky, noisy, but historic—until 2005, when Harrah's took it over and moved to the Rio out near the Las Vegas Strip. (I played poker in Binion's once—not in the WSOP—for the romance, but it's surely not my favorite venue. They do have a good deal on a steak dinner, though.)

The WSOP has garnered many tales over its lifetime. In 1972 the outcome was fixed to allow the garrulous and media-savvy Amarillo Slim to wear the crown. In 1976 and '77, Brunson took home the bacon—two years in a row—with starting hands of 10-2 that grew to full houses.

The now-famous phrase "a chip and a chair" was born in 1982. Early on Jack Straus shoved his stack of chips in, usually signifying that he was "all in" with that bet. He lost the hand. But, as he started to pick up his gear he found one more chip under his napkin, still on the table. So Straus was technically in the game—for one more hand.

He won that hand. Next hand he went all in. And won, again . . . and again. These minor wins gave Straus confidence and he became very aggressive, raising virtually every pot, eliminating one opponent after another—until the final showdown came, with Straus facing Dewey Tomko. Tomko went all in with the ace–four of diamonds; Straus called with ace-ten unsuited. The flop paired Tomko's four, the last card provided another ten for Straus, along with the pot and the title. And now you're likely to hear "a chip and a chair" at least once in every casino poker game.

The biggest boost to poker from the WSOP came in 2003. By then you could enter either by paying the normal entry fee of $10,000, or by winning one of the eligible satellite tourneys held around the country. (A local casino or Internet card room might run a competition that, with enough players, could generate a profit of over $10,000, and that amount would then go for the winner's WSOP entry fee.) The satellite reward would be a seat in the WSOP.

In 2003 Chris Moneymaker, a twenty-seven-year-old accountant from Tennessee, put down his $39 entry fee to play in a PokerStars online satellite tournament. He won and went on to take the $2.5 million first-place prize in the WSOP. Now every Tom, Diane, and Harry figured they too could parley a few dollars' buy-in to become world champion (the 2017 winner took home $8.15 million). And they tried and are still trying, by the millions. As Chris Moneymaker has said, "The beautiful thing about poker is that everybody thinks they can play."

THE MOVIES

Poker in the New West was further encouraged by its role in a range of movies; sometimes you could almost say that poker was the star. Of course, the movies consistently got some things wrong—at least regarding the rules followed in casinos today.

For example, movie characters often say, "I call your $1,000, and raise you . . ." You either call or you raise, you don't say both. Usually this kind of statement is accompanied by a "string bet." A string bet occurs when a player moves some chips into the middle of the table and then adds more in a second movement. String bets are forbidden because they might induce a following player to give away his intentions. Steve McQueen is a classic abuser in *The Cincinnati Kid*.

In all the casino games I've seen in the last several years, "table stakes" is the rule—you play with the money you have on the table. You can't go to your billfold or pocket in the middle of a hand. Nor can you call a pause, go to your room, and come back with a wad that you throw on the table. Not in the middle of a hand you don't, and in casinos you can only add money if you leave the table and get reseated someplace else.

"Slow-rolling" may not be against the rules but it is sure against the etiquette. In *Maverick* Mel Gibson turns over four cards to a royal flush, then pauses an inordinately long time before revealing the final ace. Rules like these are intended to protect all players and bring order to a game. In home games they are often willingly violated, possibly because the players are influenced by the movies.

Movies, because they're movies, are prone to plotting outrageous hands that defy any sense of a normal distribution or "law of averages." Take the final hand in *The Cincinnati Kid*—the game is five-card stud: one down, bet, one up, bet, etc., until four are up. No draws, no wild cards. The hand is dealt a card at a time with much dramatic betting, and in the showdown Steve McQueen's full house is beaten by Edward G. Robinson's straight flush. Poker pro Anthony Holden says the odds against a straight flush and a full house occurring in one hand of a two-handed game of five-card stud are more than 1 billion to 1. And to make it worse, both players bet as if they know all along what their final hands will be.

The Sting really gets into it: Paul Newman's character and Robert Shaw's both slip in stacked decks. Newman fake-shuffles and cuts, pretending to be drunk. Shaw deals Newman four treys, then triumphantly turns up four nines. Newman turns his cards over, which are supposed to be four threes as dealt, but he shows four . . . jacks: "When crook meets crook."

A few of the other movies that feature poker, mostly unrealistically, include *Rounders*, *Casino*, *Cool Hand Luke*, and, of course, *The Gambler*.

For all its appearances in film, poker has never been nominated for an Oscar. Seems narrow-minded.

Afterword

WHY THEY MOSTLY WIN
(EXCEPT FOR THOSE WHO MOSTLY LOSE)

IN THE OLD WEST, JUST LIKE TODAY, CERTAIN PLAYERS MOSTLY won (*nobody* always wins). Others, on the average and over time, lost more than they won.

In today's sociopolitical environment there are forces advocating against poker, claiming it is simply a game of chance and therefore purely gambling (though they don't oppose the stock market—often called "the big casino"—which for most investors is in reality just gambling). Devotees of poker, citing strong and thorough research, maintain that chance is a factor but the player's skill is more important.

I've played casino poker for over twenty years. At first I mostly lost. Then I studied, actually pretty hard, and also continuously gained experience. Eventually I became a consistent winner. By that I mean that my cumulative won-loss fund was positive and growing.

I'm not inherently a good poker player. It's actually pretty hard work for me, but for a number of years I enjoyed the game and the modest winnings enough to commit to the ongoing study—the work. Eventually, though, the work outweighed the pleasure, partly because the pleasure was diminished as winning (long-term) became routine. As the song says, the thrill was gone. And without enough pleasure, it was an easy decision to give up the difficult study and practice.

There are others who are willing to keep on with the work. Some even accumulate massive winnings and become famous.

Others are just so invested in the process that it becomes pretty much their life's purpose, and indeed, their life.

Some players successfully rely on the accumulation of experience, and don't bother with a lot of mathematics-based study. Such as whether to throw away a pair of aces.

Suppose, in a Texas hold 'em game, you receive two aces down—the best possible hand, *at that point*. But if several players stay until all five face-up cards are on the table, the odds of a pair of aces winning goes down and your hand becomes an underdog. Because, with several players staying until the end, *someone* is likely to end up with a full house, flush, straight, three of a kind, or even two pairs—all of which beat a pair of aces (of course, you might be one of the players who improves). And so, in such a game a pair of aces is a losing hand unless you can raise aggressively enough to drive most other players out.

The players who truly learn from experience and integrate their past experiences into their current play will be pleased to see an opening pair of aces, but, if their raising doesn't cause enough others to fold, they will throw those aces away. Those who don't really integrate their experiences, or simply don't have enough experience, will likely stay with the aces until the bitter end—bitter, because they lose.

Then there are the "naturals." These are players who seem to have a sense for what other players have as hands proceed. Yes, they closely attend to mannerisms and watch for "tells" (quirks that may give away the power of one's hand, such as tapping your fingers on the table). But that's not enough; naturals seem to almost *know*—probably not all the time, possibly only in certain circumstances—what cards others are holding. It's much like muscle memory in sports and dancing. You do what needs to be done without really thinking about it, and afterwards can't explain *how* you knew. Constant intuition?

In today's casinos it is quite difficult to come out ahead even on the average, because most casinos take 10 percent of each pot (in games with higher stakes, this "rake" is replaced with a time charge). But there are still players who make a good living playing poker. Of course, many of them also spend freely on "good living," just like they did in the Old West.

So what about the players in the Old West? I've not encountered any evidence that a Wyatt Earp or Calamity Jane dug into the mathematics of poker, and the lengthy library shelves of good books that we have today simply did not exist at that time. In research for this book I also haven't run into anyone in the Old West who claimed that they studied poker seriously, or was so described by others.

It's evident that those who made a living from poker in the Old West—a Wes Hardin or a Lottie Deno—were successful because they were good at it. Of course, a major factor in their success was probably the ineptitude of most of their opponents: cowboys, miners, trappers, soldiers whose lives were fully occupied with "real" work, but who were drawn to the saloons and card rooms for the pleasures of alcohol and companionship. Or in the case of Calamity Jane, just to be with men.

But the successful players, for whom poker was a profession, were probably poker naturals—people who might not be able to explain to you how they were able to play well and winningly, who might say they "just did it." You've undoubtedly known some like that.

So, a combination of some natural ability, an accumulation of experience that allowed a more-realistic assessment of hand likelihoods and possibilities, plus the final bounty of a never-ending supply of innocents whose alcohol consumption made them loose with their money—all of this made up the profession of poker in the Old West. And it *was* seen as a profession, in the sense that it was so viewed and accepted in society. Never by everyone, of course, but usually by those whose opinions you might care about.

Gambling was an unfavorable catchall term that included all those obsessive persons who would keep betting on the horses, on faro, on roulette, until the money was all gone—including the grocery money, the rent money, the baby's milk money. So while "gambling" was bad, in the Old West, professional poker players were skilled individuals with an acceptable career.

Appendix A

GAMES PEOPLE PLAYED

In poker today the hand ranking order is well established. In the Old West some of these hands were not recognized;
for instance, in the earlier days, straights weren't counted.

Here's how poker hands are ranked:

- Five of a kind: This is only possible with at least one wild
  card. I haven't been in every casino in the world, but I've
  never encountered a casino game with wild cards.
- Royal flush, ten-jack-queen-king-ace all of one suit: This is
  the highest-ranking hand unless there are wild cards.
- Straight flush, five cards in sequence all of one suit (e.g.,
  six-seven-eight-nine-ten of hearts)
- Four of a kind, four cards of a single rank (e.g., three of
  spades, three of clubs, three of diamonds, three of hearts,
  plus any other card)
- Full house, a "boat": This is three of one rank, two of
  another; often described as, for example, "eights full,"
  meaning a full house topped by three eights and another
  pair. "Aces full" is of course a very strong hand.
- Flush, five cards of a single suit (e.g., all clubs)
- Straight, five cards in unbroken sequence (e.g., nine through
  king)
- Trips, or three of a kind: This is three of a single rank plus
  two other (unpaired) cards.

- Two pairs (not "two pair"), such as jack-jack, six-six, plus any other card. Hickok's aces and eights were two pairs.
- One pair plus three other cards
- High card: When no one has a higher hand, the one with the highest card wins; ace is of course the highest possible card, but any card will qualify so long as no one has a higher one. If two hands show the same high card, highest second card in those two hands will be the winner (suits are not ranked).

Betting in poker often can include anything. Antes are common; these are fixed, required bets before any cards are dealt. So a game might require every player to put one chip (or a nickel, or any amount the players may agree on) into the pot before play begins.

"Table stakes" is often a declared rule, but sometimes implied. In table stakes, a player can bet only with the money or chips he or she has on the table before the hand begins.

FIVE-CARD STUD

Players receive one card down and four up; at the end of the deal players can see four-fifths (or 80 percent) of every hand. The deal goes this way:

- Everyone antes.
- One card is dealt facedown all around, one card faceup, then a round of betting ensues.
- The dealer deals another card faceup, and then another round of betting ensues. These steps are repeated twice more.
- After five cards have been dealt, with four showing for each hand, the final betting round occurs.
- When all players have either folded or called the last bet, the down card of the last bettor/raiser is exposed. However,

if no one has called the last bettor or raiser, that player is entitled to the pot without having to reveal the down card. In other words, "Ya gotta pay to see it."

I've been in games in which no one called the last bettor; as he was raking in the pot, another player reached over and exposed the winner's down card. War almost ensued. Don't do it.

In the Old West five-card stud was it until five-card draw came along.

FIVE-CARD DRAW

Players ante, then receive five cards facedown. There's a round of betting, and then each player examines his/her hand and decides to:

- Stand pat, and play the original five cards with no replacements. This suggests a very strong hand that can't be improved, such as a full house, flush, or straight. But it could just be a bluff.

- Draw one: Players holding two pairs, four of a single suit (which might become a flush with one more card—odds against it happening are 5.78 to 1), or "four to a straight" (four cards within a five-card connected sequence, but missing one card to be a straight—on average this will happen once in 5.88 times, about 6 to 1 against, worse if one of the four cards is an ace). Most players would typically throw away the extra card and draw one, but the bettor could also be lying/bluffing (thus, the origin of the term "four flusher").

- Draw two: Those drawing two are generally presumed to be holding three of a kind, trips. But I have encountered crazy hopefuls ("It *could* happen") who hold, say, three to a flush and hopefully draw two (odds of that becoming a flush are 25 to 1 against—it'll happen on average only once in 25 tries). Odds against filling a three-card straight are even worse, 135 to 1 against.

- Draw three: This usually means the player has nothing, but you would also draw three if you were dealt one pair. I suppose one could hold two of a suit with the hope that you would draw three more of that suit to get a flush—odds against this happening are 135 to 1; similarly with two to a straight.

Usually in five-card draw three cards is the maximum number that can be drawn. Home games may allow more, including the possibility of drawing five—throwing your whole hand away, taking a chance that five new cards will be better. Some home games allow a sequence of draws—first three, then two, then one.

The draw is followed by a last round of betting, followed by the showdown. Usually this means that all players still in the hand at the end turn over their cards so the winner can be determined. But, if there is a bet or raise in the last round and no one calls it, that bettor wins the pot and is not required to reveal the hand.

A popular version of five-card draw, jacks or better, is designed to bring a bit of order to the game by requiring a minimum hand before one is allowed to open the betting, thus eliminating wild betting and bluffing on the first round of betting before the draw.

JACKS OR BETTER (ALSO "JACKPOTS," SOMETIMES SIMPLY "JACKS")

This is a game of five-card draw in which the opening hand must contain jacks or better. After the five cards have been dealt and the round of betting begins, a player is not allowed to open the betting, to be the first bettor, unless holding a hand with a pair of jacks or something higher. Other players may then call or raise regardless of what's in their hand, recognizing of course that they are going up against at least a pair of jacks.

Often no one will be able to open, so players then re-ante (an additional ante) and a new round begins. Sometimes several deals will occur before anyone can open, resulting in an opening pot that might contain twenty or more antes.

Who polices the jacks-or-better rule? Usually the other players themselves are responsible for determining that the opener has met that condition. If the opener happens to win the pot, *and* if no one has called on the final round, it may be necessary for the winning hand to be exposed so all can see whether it at least contains jacks or better. In this one case other players are entitled to see at least part (two jacks) of the winning hand without having "paid to see it."

EUCHRE

This game isn't seen much today, but it was popular during the Old West days. In fact, it was once the most popular trump game in America.

It was seen as sociable, nonthreatening (it was played for points, with money usually not involved), and relatively civilized—a characteristic especially appealing to "gentlemen" on the riverboats. For these several reasons it was seen by professional gamblers as a useful lead-in to a lucrative game of poker. After playing for points awhile, the pro would suggest a bet on a hand—and then would soon propose a change to poker.

There are many variations, but the basic game has two partnerships of two players each. A deck of twenty-four cards is used, nines through aces (later thirty-two cards, sevens through aces). Five cards are dealt to each player, with the remaining four stacked in the middle, and the top card faceup as the potential trump.

Players "bid" by announcing, in effect, that they can take at least three tricks and they want the top card's suit to be trumps; the up card then goes into the dealer's, not the bidder's, hand, who must discard one. One point is awarded for each trick taken. The bidding player/team must win at least three tricks; otherwise, two points are awarded to their opponents. Five points wins the game.

I won't go into all the details, but we can note that euchre was popular because it was fast and allowed for the exercise of a degree of skill. It was closer to bridge than to poker, but as noted, professional gamblers were adept at leading players from a game of euchre to a money game of poker.

Euchre gave us some interesting terms: jack of trumps was the "right bower," or highest-ranking card; the other jack of the same color (for example, if hearts was trumps, then the other red jack, of diamonds) was "left bower," or second-highest ranking; the joker was called the "best bower" but was, in fact, not the *best* bower—it was the third-ranking card. And "euchred" came to refer to being deceived or cheated; a player was said to have been euchred when another managed to prevent him or her from being able to take three tricks.

Faro

Faro—originally "pharaoh" and then "pharo"—can be traced to France in the 1600s. As the Old West developed, faro naturally rode along. It was easy to learn and gave a fast play; and, in an honest game, the odds were better than in most other gambling games. Hamlet would say, "Aye, there's the rub."

Faro could accommodate any number of players. Bets were placed on a board that contained a representation of one complete suit of cards, ace through king. Bets were placed on the individual cards in the layout. Multiple bets were allowed.

The deck would be shuffled and placed in a "shoe," or box. One card was then drawn and placed to the right; this was called the "banker's card." A second card, the "player's card," was placed to the left.

Then the bets were settled. Bets on the player's card would win even money (one chip returns one more chip). Bets on the banker's card lost. When both of the two cards were the same rank, the dealer took half of each bet and returned the remainder to the player; in other words, the player lost half his bet. This was the main basis of the dealer's advantage.

Different betting occurred on the order of the last three cards; predicting the exact order paid five to one. Odds were important because you were playing against the "house," the dealer. (Odds weren't relevant, at least in the same way, in poker; odds exist for the likelihood of being dealt a particular hand, but poker is played against other gamblers, not against the house.)

Obviously serious or thoughtful players would want to keep track of the cards previously turned, so they could figure out how many of each rank were left (e.g., if four jacks have already been turned, you don't want to put your money on the jack). To avoid having, say, ten bettors each keeping a running count, a casekeeper was part of the game. This person tallied the cards on a device called a "casekeep," which looked like an abacus with beads on wires. All players could glance at the casekeep in deciding how they would bet.

Odds in a fair game of faro were as favorable—or more accurately, the least unfavorable—to the player as any table game in the Old West.

But techniques for cheating were soon developed. The dealing box, or shoe, was an attractive possibility; sporting-house companies quickly began offering specially rigged dealing boxes to saloons and would-be faro bankers. Cheating became so prevalent, in fact, that an edition of *Hoyle's Rules of Games* warned that it was not possible to find an honest faro bank in the United States. But still they kept playing.

Some of the notable poker players in the Old West, like Wild Bill Hickok, Doc Holliday, and John Wesley Hardin, were virtually obsessed with faro. They would take their poker winnings to the faro table and quickly lose all. This attitude was perhaps best articulated by Canada Bill, a cohort of George Devol on the Mississippi steamboats. In a small Louisiana town he found a faro game in the back room of a barbershop. Bill's partner quickly spotted the crooked dealer's box and urged Bill to walk away. Bill's response? "I can't. It's the only game in town."

(Canada Bill worked with George Devol, who described him as "a character one might travel the length and breadth of the land and never find his match." Devol describes him as "a medium-sized, chicken-headed, tow-haired sort of a man" who dressed poorly and never weighed more than 130 pounds. He also looked slow-witted—he "resembled an idiot"—but that was all an act, a put-on that Bill was the sucker when in fact the sucker was whoever he could fool into making that misjudgment.)

Players could also cheat, but it was more difficult and could be more easily detected—with potentially lethal consequences.

Faro continued until after World War II, when it became scarce except in Las Vegas.

Monte

There was only one *game* of monte, and it wasn't "three-card monte."

Three-card monte is not a game; it is purely, and always, a scam. This seductive hustle can be encountered even today on the streets of cities such as San Francisco, Chicago, and New York. (A full description is given in appendix C, "How They Cheated.")

The other monte, the genuine gambling game, was practically the national game of Mexico in the days of the Old West; hence, it was often identified as Mexican monte, also called monte bank.

The game was played with forty cards, minus the eights, nines, and tens. Four cards are laid out faceup, two from the top of the deck for the "top layout," and two from the bottom of the deck for the "bottom layout." (Another version had only one card each in the top and bottom layouts, with lower odds for the players.) Bets are placed on either the top layout or the bottom, without regard to which specific card the bet was on. So if you wanted to bet a dollar on the bottom layout, you would place your dollar or chip on one—either one—of the cards in the bottom layout.

Next the whole deck is turned over so the bottom card is faceup. This is called the "gate" card. If the suit of the gate card matches the suit of *either* card in the top layout, bets on the top layout win and are paid one to one. The same goes for the bottom layout. If you bet on the bottom layout, and the suit of the gate card matches the suit of one of the bottom layout cards, you win.

Monte's appeal was that it was very fast, more so than faro and much more so than poker. Dealing was quick and easy, which is why Madame Vestal, Doña Tules, and Billy the Kid liked to deal it. If you wanted to get your money into play quickly, over and over, you'd head for the monte table. And many did.

A fair monte game had only a 3 percent dealer advantage— and a fair monte game was probably about as scarce as a soft-hearted prostitute. A deck of handheld cards was, for a good card mechanic, easy to manipulate. There's no machine or dealer's box to examine, and certainly (in those days) no video of the hand just passed. Thus any argument was quickly ignored as the other players rushed to get down their bets and the dealer rushed into the next deal.

A good example of monte cheating is given in Charles L. Convis's *Gamblers* (Pioneer Press, 2000). Texas gambler Ben Thompson, at the time a soldier, was dealing a monte game in Laredo for a bunch of Mexican soldiers. Thompson had amassed $1,800, but now the men were getting agitated, mean. Thompson spotted one of them palming a card. In this version of monte, Thompson would lay out two cards, players would bet on one or the other, and Thompson would deal through the deck until he matched one of the turned-up cards. Betting was normal until he laid out a seven and a four; all the bets were placed on the seven, none on the four.

To Thompson it was obvious that the card palmed had been a four. With only two fours left in the deck, versus three sevens, odds were three to two on the seven, and that's where the bets had landed.

Thompson asked the saloon-keeper for a new deck while easing his winnings into a canvas bag. The soldiers, guessing that their game had been detected, began to push in on him. A tall lieutenant growled, "Mr. Ben, you can't close this game." Thompson replied, "The game is closed."

The lieutenant pulled his gun, swiping at one of the two candles lighting the room as he did so. Another soldier drew and shot at Thompson and missed; Thompson then shot him in the head and shot the lieutenant in the chest, blew out the second candle, and dived into an alcove partly hidden by an open door. He later counted eight shots in the door, but he wasn't hit.

In the ensuing confusion Thompson tried to mingle with the crowd, but a soldier spotted him and let fly with a shotgun. Pellets punctured his coat as he dived into a pond. He was able to swim underwater to the far bank. He crawled out, shaking the water out of his hair, and landed almost in the middle of a Mexican cavalry unit. The troop commander wanted to know what was going on across the pond, and what Thompson was doing in the pond. Ben replied that he was just taking an evening swim (fully clothed?) and the fellows across the pond were just having some fun with a brother. As the cavalry rode off, Thompson hid in a cemetery. Later he crept to the Rio Grande and floated, with the aid of some sagebrush, for two miles.

Eventually Thompson made it back to his own army unit, only slightly the worse for wear.

Pitch, Old Sledge, Seven-Up

These are all various names for a bidding game, with trumps, that is somewhat similar to euchre. Such games might be attractive to players who were low on (or out of) cash, or who just didn't care to gamble. It does seem, however, that in the Old West there were few who fit the latter category.

Appendix B

MODERN POKER GAMES

SEVEN-CARD STUD

It's difficult to definitively trace the origin of seven-card stud, but it wasn't played in the Old West before the Civil War, and, from what records exist, it doesn't appear to have been popular during the cowboy era. But through most of the twentieth century seven-card stud ruled, mostly displacing five-card stud. Players could see more of others' hands, and there were more betting rounds, which meant bigger pots.

The hand goes like this:

- Everyone antes.
- Three cards are dealt around, two facedown and the last faceup, followed by a first round of betting.
- Another card is dealt faceup, followed by betting.
- This is repeated until all players still in the hand have received four face-up cards.
- The last card, the "river" card (don't ask me where that label came from) is dealt facedown. There's a concluding round of betting, then the showdown.

Seven-card stud grew in popularity until it was by far the most popular version of poker played in the United States.

But another form of stud was developing. As the Texas Road Gamblers spread their play throughout Texas in the 1960s, this new game, Texas hold 'em, was pretty much their main game.

TEXAS HOLD 'EM

This game *may have* started in Texas—nobody seems to know for sure. Robstown is sometimes cited as its birthplace. All we really know is that it became popular in that state during the 1960s and was introduced to Las Vegas, Nevada, in 1967.

Texas hold 'em and the World Series of Poker sort of developed together. After the first year of the series, in 1970, the main game became, and has always remained, Texas hold 'em. Eventually the World Series of Poker was televised and poker's popularity began to rise.

Why did hold 'em become so popular?

As I've noted elsewhere in this book, it has two attractive, if competing, attributes. Pros like it as a highly complex game with ample opportunities for application of strategy and psychology. Tyros like it as a simple game in which you can see most of everyone's cards. They are both right—sort of. But the pros are more right.

Play goes like this:

- Each hold 'em game has a betting label, such as "$5–$10 fixed limit" or "$1–$2 no limit." In fixed limit, bets are in fixed increments; in this case, $10. In a no-limit game players may bet anything up to the total amount they have on the table at the start of the hand.

- When a game starts, a "dealer" is chosen randomly. This person doesn't do any dealing; it's just a label and a place marker. With each new hand, the dealer marker is moved one seat to the left.

- The next player to the "dealer's" left is called the small blind. This person must post (bet) before the first card of a hand is dealt, a small amount ($5 in a $5–$10 game). Next player to the left is the big blind, who must post the larger amount, $10 in a $5–$10 game. (Blinds move one seat to the left with each new hand, staying ahead of the "dealer" marker.) These blind requirements serve, instead of antes, to get some money in the pot at the start of a hand as an inducement to other players to become involved. Without any money in the pot to start, or any cost of continuously playing without betting, some players would monotonously fold every hand until they received what they perceived to be winning cards.

- The deal begins with each player receiving two cards facedown, or "in the hole," followed by a round of betting.

- Next, three cards are placed faceup near the middle of the table. This is called the "flop"; these and subsequent face-up cards are available to every player. Another round of betting occurs.

- The next round is called the "turn." One more card is placed faceup alongside the flop, and then a round of betting follows.

- The final round, the "river," is one card faceup with the other four. All players who are still in the hand can now form their best hand from their two hole cards *and* the five up cards. Of course, all players can see the five exposed cards, so it is often possible to determine the best possible hand that could be formed (*could*, depending on the quality of one's hole cards). There is a final round of betting, hole cards are exposed by the last bettor or raiser, and the pot winner is determined.

For most of the twentieth century, seven-card stud dominated the poker tables. With the advent of the World Series of Poker's emphasis on Texas hold 'em, that game began to edge out stud.

When I began playing in casinos in the early 1990s, both games were common. Gradually, though, stud began to disappear. In the last few years you would have to search diligently in casinos for a stud game, which is too bad; like many others, I enjoy stud more.

OMAHA

Omaha didn't figure at all in the Old West, but came into play in the early 1980s—and not in Omaha, Nebraska, either.

The game is, on the surface, quite similar to hold 'em, but played with four hole cards. You have the same three-card deal (flop), then a turn card and the river. Two additional changes are common: You must use exactly two of your four hole cards in forming your best hand, and the game is almost always played high-low.

High-low means that, at the final showdown in a hand, the pot is usually divided between the best high hand and the best low hand. If the game is played "eights or better," it means to qualify as a low hand there can be no card larger than an eight. There are different ways of defining the best low hand, so players should be sure they know the rules and protocol for any unfamiliar game.

My exposure with Omaha went like this: It was one of those questionable venues, my first time there, and I was already uncomfortable. The only game available was a combination of hold 'em and Omaha, alternating (allegedly) each time around the table—i.e., every eight or nine hands.

So I asked someone, "How do you play Omaha?"

"Oh, it's just like hold 'em, except you start with four hole cards."

How hard could that be? I thought. And I can sit out most of the Omaha deals, waiting for hold 'em to come around.

Except it never came around.

I asked the dealer about it, and he brushed me off with something like, "Oh, we'll get to it." But they didn't get to it soon enough, for I managed to lose my entire stake without seeing a hold 'em hand. I tried to think of it as a learning experience. But—I hadn't *learned* anything. I was befuddled the whole time, which is pretty much what the experienced players count on.

They especially like the confusion over the rule that you must use exactly two cards from your hand. So, say you get dealt three hearts and happily look for two hearts to fall on the board, to fill your hand into a flush. Except—you can use only two of your hole cards in forming your hand, so that third heart is useless; you would only have four to a flush (two in your hand, two on the board).

Eventually I did learn a bit more and came to enjoy Omaha myself. But don't be fooled. While it may look simple, it's anything but.

Appendix C

HOW THEY CHEATED

"STOP CHEATING!" THE DEALER TOLD THE CARD PLAYER.

"I'm not!" claimed the player.

"You must be," said the dealer. "That's not the hand I dealt you!"

As long as there have been, and as long as there will be, card games played for money, there will be cheating. Among the professional gamblers in the Old West were those who prided themselves on playing fair, and there were also those who viewed fairness as a sucker's play. Even if you thought cheating was weak and inappropriate, to protect yourself you had to know the cheaters' devices and ploys. In other words, you had to be fully versed in all the techniques of cheating even if you didn't personally engage in it yourself.

Americans in the nineteenth century were demonstrably gamblers, trekking westward over unknown lands in search of—what? Fortune, adventure, battle, "a chance"; by ship, wagon, horseback and muleback, "shank's mare" (foot), stagecoach. By rudimentary, rough, and rattle-y trains subject to frequent derailment or hold-ups by bandits.

Southerners were even more likely to take risks. Males particularly, in the slaveholding, plantation-oriented culture, grew to adulthood with role models that prized chance-taking as "manly," with the concomitant standard that a gentleman takes his losses with a smile and a shrug and never a look back. In other words, they were perfect candidates for the poker table.

Most gambling involves choosing how, when, and what amount to bet against the house (blackjack, dice with a house setup, Spanish monte, faro), device (roulette), or game (horse racing, keno, sports). Occasionally the bettor has a chance to exploit ignorance about odds (e.g., "home" dice games). This is always true in poker, but most importantly in poker, the bettor is going against other players, other humans with their own decision-making skills, or lack thereof. Poker is about the only type of gambling that involves this competition between humans. This is the reason many say that poker is not gambling per se but rather a game of skill. (A weakness in this argument is that, unquestionably, luck is a significant factor. But not always: I once played in a poker game in New Mexico in which one very aggressive player bragged he could win without looking at his cards, and then proceeded to do so for seven straight hands. Or as modern poker behemoth Phil Helmuth is prone to say, "If it wasn't for luck I'd win every hand.")

Okay, so poker is more a game of skill than of luck. But that won't matter very much if there are good cheaters—sharpers—at the table.

I could review the cheating methods common today, but they might not be relevant to the days of the Old West. It is more appropriate to discuss the methods in use back then. Therefore, I'm relying on a contemporary book, *Sharps and Flats: A Complete Revelation of the Secrets of Cheating at Games of Chance and Skill* by John Nevil Maskelyne, published in 1894.

WAYS TO CHEAT

One of the simpler, yet effective, cheating methods is to have spotters—"onlookers" who position themselves to be able to read players' cards and communicate their holdings to a partner at the table.

Devol ran into a spotter setup when he visited an Indian camp. Indians, Devol was told, were often good poker players, and they were always "looking for the best of it." That sounded like they might be looking for some kind of advantage, and that was right up Devol's alley. He loved to give an apparent advantage, usually by stacking or marking the cards.

So, Devol hired a horse and buggy and headed west from St. Paul looking for Indians, which he soon found. After a friendly pipe and some palaver, a poker game was started. Right off Devol spotted the poker-playing chief cheating by using a sliver of mirror embedded inside an old hat. Devol warned him to put the hat away, but then a young man started walking around behind the poker players, making big talk. He was peeping at the hands as he passed behind each player and sending hand signals to the chief. Devol waited until he was dealt a strong hand, four fives and a jack, which he then slid up his sleeve to wait until the betting warmed up.

Soon the chief got a good hand and started betting strongly; Devol raised right back. His present cards were mediocre, and he handled them casually enough for the young spy to get a good look. He then shifted the four fives from his sleeve into his hand. He kept this hidden from the spy, of course.

Devol pushed in a pile of silver, the chief called, and Devol won the showdown. The chief leapt up, grabbed his tomahawk, and went after the young spotter, who wisely hightailed it for the tall timber.

Devol whipped off his coat, dumped the pile of silver into it, jumped into his buggy, and laid on the whip. Looking back, he could see the chief closing in on the heels of the desperate young scamp.

MARKED CARDS

Most people seem to believe that, presented with a deck of cards known to be marked, they could spot the marking. But if the marking was done by a professional card engineer, you or I are almost certainly not going to be able to detect it.

Houdini tried. A cardsharper had been caught cheating, and authorities found a quantity of cards in his possession. Not being skilled at identifying marked cards, they asked Houdini to examine them. He agreed readily, figuring he would take some pleasure in exposing the cheat. He studied the cards carefully, with a magnifying glass, reflected light, lenses and light that detect invisible ink, holding and riffling them at all angles. Weeks passed, and Houdini was frustrated; irritated, he flung the deck across the room—and immediately spotted the marking.

As the tossed cards moved through a sunlit area, a small place on the back of each card did not glisten; the glaze had been removed. This would have been easy for the cheater to read; a drop of water would have done it, blotted up after a few seconds. Completely invisible under ordinary circumstances, but visible when the cards were held at a suitable angle to the light.

With unglazed cards, the opposite approach could be used by adding glaze markings that would only be visible when the light was at the right angle, easy enough for a dealer to obtain as the cards are handled.

Various methods using ink were common. Dots, thickened lines, slight filling of an angle's vertex, shading, and tinting were all successfully applied. The nonexpert will rarely be able to even tell *whether* cards have been marked, much less interpret the meanings of the permutations of a particular style.

(To mark a deck, a thin metal plate is first prepared, the same shape and size as a card, with small holes drilled in the plate at locations that will identify the card rank and suit. The plate is laid over each card and a needle is lightly applied in the hole appropriate for each card's identity.)

Lightly shaved edges, detectable in an expert's hands while shuffling, can be effective. Pricking the front of a card will cause a small bump to be raised on the back. Bumps might have been detectable by Houdini, but in a normal poker game they would be unnoticed by all but the sharper.

Most of these methods require prior preparation, and in fact pre-marked cards are available from manufacturers. But marking can even take place while the cards are in play. For pricking, one method is to use a ring which has a small point extending from the bottom—that is, the palm side of the finger. This point would be rather short, perhaps ⅟₆₄th of an inch, and thus essentially invisible to other players.

Tinting can be applied during a game. One method involves the prior preparation of a cork in which a small hole is scooped, then filled with a colored paste; the cork may then be sewn into the seam of a coat or vest. The color will virtually match the color of the pattern on the back of the cards. During a game the operator will rub a finger on the paste, then apply it delicately to the back of selected cards, slightly deepening the tint in the spot to which it is applied.

Preparation of two pastes, one blue and one red, would permit the accomplished cheater to deal with almost any deck.

REFLECTORS

Reflectors of various sorts have been applied and may be encountered at any time. Small reflectors can be built into snuff boxes, pipes, lighters, pens, rings, and any of the small devices, including "keepsake" casino chips, placed on top of one's hand to "protect" the cards from being mucked by the dealer.

Mirrors may be secreted under a table (affixed to be swung out for use, and then back out of sight) or in various walls around the room. A drop of wine, carelessly spilled on the table, has even been used. Or a confederate might be enlisted.

We visited master cheater George Devol earlier. One of his gambits involved an old steamboat that was tied up at Baton Rouge, serving as a lodging house. Devol rented a stateroom next to the adjoining gambling parlor. Then he and his partner bored a hole in the floor under the poker table where Devol would sit, another hole under one of the beds in the stateroom next door, and a third one in the wall or bulkhead of the stateroom. From here the partner could lie in the berth and look out into the gambling room, reading the cards of the players with their backs to him.

Next they would affix a nail into a spring, and fasten the spring on the underside of the floor beneath Devol's seat at the poker table. A wire was run from the spring into the stateroom. With one boot off and the stockinged foot on the nail, Devol could read signals from his partner—three tugs, for example, meant the mark was holding three of a kind. Then Devol would line up a promising mark and get him seated at a table with his back to the stateroom.

It worked fine until the partner dozed off in the berth. Devol waited without any signals for as long as he could, then picked up a spittoon and threw it against the stateroom wall (Devol told the other players that he was just mad because his cards were running bad). This woke the partner, and the signal system promptly resumed.

Holdouts

Holdouts assist the operator in secreting a card, usually on the person but sometimes under the table. Those made for the body can range from the fairly simple, such as a clip and spring on a rod up a sleeve, to an elaborate series of hinges and rods that may be actuated, for example, by moving a foot. Reading a comprehensive description of alternative models can be as challenging as reading a full text on automobile mechanics.

But being smooth with a holdout might not suffice. One fellow was following his usual practice of slipping an ace up his sleeve. As he waited for the appropriate hand in which to add his hideaway ace, he surveyed the table and realized that he was in the midst of some very dangerous men—and they were eyeing him keenly. This led to the hasty conclusion that he did not want to have that ace in his sleeve if anyone decided to challenge him.

But he was cool and above all a survivor, as he would have to have been to not get caught and maybe killed over his practices. He casually ordered a sandwich from the bar. As he started eating, and was of course out of the hand, he noted that the gunmen were concentrating on the game and not on him. So he gently slid the ace into his sandwich—and then continued eating until the sandwich and ace were both gone. He didn't get to use the ace, but he did get to live for future games.

Holdouts don't have to be complicated to be effective. A simple table holdout is thus described by its manufacturer: "Very small and light. It can be put under and removed from any table in less than half a minute. Works easily from either knee. It will bring three or more cards up into your hand and take back the discards as you hold your hands and cards in a natural position on top of the table."

CARD MANIPULATION

Finally, card decks, even if unmarked, can be arranged so the operator can know what others are holding. Pre-stacking a new deck, then rewrapping and sealing it in a card box (with a counterfeit tax seal, of course), has been mentioned in this book. The operator when dealing will call for a new deck, and (following prior bribery) will be provided with his stacked deck by the runner or bartender.

Really competent cardsharps don't even need to pre-stack. They have the ability to arrange an entire deck to their satisfaction right before your eyes.

Simpler methods are readily mastered by even "amateur" sharps. Second-dealing (the card after the top card), bottom dealing, and fake shuffling or cutting (going through motions that appear to be real but leave the deck unchanged) may sound easy to spot, but I've sat in front of a good card mechanic who told me exactly what he was going to do, and I still couldn't spot him doing it.

In a word, never underestimate the ability of an expert card mechanic or sharper.

It was on a pleasant trip from Memphis to Natchez back in the steamboat days. As the supper tables were cleared, a couple of poker games started up, and one soon involved higher stakes, with several thousand dollars in sight. Watchers began to gather 'round, including a striking woman traveling alone.

Most of the female travelers were conservatively dressed, but this lady, recognized by a few as "Flash Kate" from New Orleans, was garbed in striking clothing with ostentatious jewelry, and she carried herself accordingly. As the game progressed and the betting amounts grew, Kate moved in closer; she appeared transfixed, her lips parted, her eyes sparkling.

Eventually a player said he'd lost enough, and retired to his cabin. Since Kate was obviously so interested in the game, she was invited to take a seat and promptly laid a handful of money on the table. Soon Keene, one of the professional players, stealthily slid an ace into his sleeve. Some onlookers spotted it, but not a word was said, since interference in that day and place meant a fight. When the deal passed to Downing, a cattle dealer from Texas, he gathered up the cards, pitched them on the floor, and called to the boat's clerk, "Bring us a fresh deck, of another color." (You couldn't very well slip an old ace into a new deck if the backs were a different color.)

Downing had obviously seen Keene's maneuver but said nothing more. He just shuffled and dealt from the new deck as if nothing unusual had happened. But with Kate now joining the game, Downing figured that she plus Keene and another professional, a Mr. Alcott, were in cahoots. Sure enough, he soon detected that they were stacking the cards as they began dealing him excellent hands. So, playing dumb, Downing kept his bets low for a while.

Then Downing pulled one of the slickest tricks ever. It was Keene's deal and Downing's cut, but by this time Keene had lost his nerve and had not set up the cards. Waiting for such a chance, Downing leaned over to cut the cards and smoothly substituted another pack, a deck he had previously stacked, for the one Keene had shuffled. This may sound impossible, but it's not uncommon with a true sleight-of-hand artist—and Downing was among the best. No player detected the substitution, and Downing would now know, for one hand, every card dealt to each player.

The game was five-card draw poker. After the draw the players all had strong hands—of course, since Downing's deck had been carefully prepared. With Keene dealing they figured it was a fair deal, so they bet their hands confidently. The pot mushroomed.

At the showdown Keene had four jacks, Alcott, four queens, Kate, four kings—and Downing showed four aces. A stunned silence! Alcott and Keene both grabbed for the money—but Downing's right hand was already pointing a derringer at them, while his left coolly pulled in the pot.

"That was no square deal!" shouted Alcott.

"Thank not?" drawled Downing. "Well, you ought to know. Your pal dealt the cards. As for me, I reckon this pot'll do me." As the swindlers slunk away, Downing turned to the crowd, ordered champagne all around, and announced, "Those three were slick, but I can show them some fellows who'll teach them what *slick* really means."

If some of the methods of cheating seem like a lot of work, remember that the professional cheater will have practiced the use of the preferred method(s) many times over, until their application is so easy in practice as to be unnoticeable by the rest of us.

Does this mean that we are always more or less at the mercy of a sharp? Others may disagree, but for me the answer is yes. The only protection is to play in a casino where dealers and floor persons are professionally trained to spot and deal with sharpers, or to be sure the stakes are low when outside a casino.

Even the old-time Texas Road Gamblers had to be constantly on the alert for cheats, and their best protection (along with a .38 Special) was to master many cheating methods themselves so they could spot and counter them.

We come now not to a particular method for cheating in, say, poker, but to a procedure that in its entirety is a cheat.

Three-Card Monte

Many think this is just another type of monte, a legitimate game. It's not, and as far as I know, has never been. It's a scam, a con, a hustle.

The western Indians had a game that resembled three-card monte. Three bones were used, two white and one red. The person whose turn it was to be the operator would rapidly shift the bones between his hands, and bettors would select the hand they thought contained the red bone. Odds should be about even money except for some advantage to the bettor who might be able to follow the red bone's movement. Cheating would have been conceivable but not too likely.

Three-card monte is similar to the bones game, except that cheating is *always* involved. It's more closely modeled after thimblerig. In that hustle, the operator places a pea under one of three shells on a flat surface. The shells are shifted quickly several times, the pea is revealed, and the moves are repeated. Onlookers can easily follow the pea and become convinced they will be able to spot which shell it is under. The operator calls for bets, a watcher puts down a bet, the shells are shifted, the bettor picks his shell and . . . no pea under it. Of course what the watchers don't know is that the pea has been dropped into the operator's lap and isn't under any shell.

With three-card monte three playing cards are used, one of which is distinctly different from the other two—perhaps a queen of spades versus two non-face cards. The cards are shifted, an onlooker points to a card, it *is* the queen of spades. This is repeated, now with the onlooker (the operator's shill) betting. The apparent bettor again identifies the black queen, and pockets the winning.

If an innocent watcher is anxious to bet, the operator accepts the bet, shifts the cards, lays them out, the bettor confidently taps one, operator turns it over . . . you lose; not the queen of spades.

Watchers and bettors tend to be continuously shifting, with new ones coming in, disappointed losers leaving, and the scam goes on. If bettors become reluctant, a new wrinkle is introduced. The operator, in shifting the cards, drops one to the floor, then bends over to pick it up. The shill slightly bends up the corner of the queen of spades and the operator resumes shifting the cards, apparently never noticing the bent corner.

Now, the onlookers can see a sure thing—just pick the card with the barely bent corner. The bet, this time probably a considerably larger one after the operator has used his verbal skills to get it up, goes down, the cards are shifted and laid out, the bettor picks the one with the bent corner, it's turned over . . . and, yep, it's *not* the queen of spades. How can that be, the bettor is wondering, as he or she shuffles away.

Possibly because the operator is highly skilled. And, the operator is a very effective spieler. Here's an actual example—imagine a very rapid patter:

Who will play me? The Ace of Spades. That is the card. The Ace of Spades, it flies through my hands. It is here, and here, now here. Do not be fooled. My hands are quicker than your eyes. The Ace of Spades. It is gone, no, it is here. The Ace of Spades is always here. All I can do is move it. Can you follow it? Twenty dollars is the bet. Is this it, no, this, yes, the Ace of Spades. Who will bet me? You only have to pick the Ace of Spades. It is one card out of three. I have two chances to your one. Follow, follow my hands, the Ace of Spades, I move it up, and down, it is always here. You watch it, you find it, you win. You win, I lose. But my hands are fast. The Ace of Spades. It is always in front of you. On the table, the Ace of Spades. There are no tricks, it is simple. You name the Ace of Spades, you win. You name another card, I win. Always fair, always open, everyone can see my every movement. I do not hide. The Ace of Spades. Ah, it is stubborn. Is it here—no! Here? Yes! Simple game. You pick, you win. I take my chances. I have two chances to your one. You have your eyes. Are they as fast as my hands?

You can see. No tricks. The Ace of Spades. You watch it, you pick it, you win, your twenty dollars is forty dollars. But I have my hands, that is all I have. Sometimes I win. Sometimes I lose. Good eyes, always win. Twenty is the bet. Do you watch or do you play? This is the game. Twenty dollars get forty. Follow the Ace of Spades, you win, I lose.

The con artist speaks rapidly, a mesmerizing singsong, repetitive. It looks so easy that most folks who are unfamiliar with three-card monte are convinced they can win, and their twenty dollars goes onto the table. And unless the dealer lets them win to entice others, the money is quickly gone.

A different, somewhat calmer approach was followed with great success by George Devol throughout his years as a riverboat hustler. His account, included in *Forty Years a Gambler on the Mississippi* (1847), shows that Devol was not only a master of three-card monte but also pretty good at human psychology.

I was on board the steamer Great Republic *at one time when there was a number of English lads among the passengers and we all got to drinking. Pretty soon my partner comes in (we pretended not to know each other), pulls out a set of tickets [cards] and starts flipping three-card monte with one of the lads. While we were drinking my partner put a crimp in the baby ticket, but took good care that the English lad saw him do it. [At this point I think Devol is the dealer.] Then he wanted me to bet money on the game, and I said: "I have two chances to your one, and could win all your money if we would bet."*

The Englishman laughed, and said: "Why, lad, you 'aven't a bloody bit of a chance; you would lose every hlarsted cent you 'ave if you bet."

My partner kept bantering me, when I pulled out a roll of greenbacks that made them open their eyes, saying: "I would not be one bit afraid to wager all that."

The Englishman gave me a nudge and said: "Lad, don't you do it."

My partner then said: "I haven't got one-half so much money, but I will bet you $500 I can pick up the baby ticket."

We put our money in the Englishman's hand, and I turned to him and offered to bet him a bottle of wine that I would win the money. He took me up. My partner turned the card, and I lost the money and the wine.

He wanted to bet me $1,000, but I told him he was a little too lucky for me. I saw Johnnie Bull was crazy to bet, so I said to him: "Do you think you could guess the baby ticket?"

"Indeed I do," he replied.

"I will wager you that you can't."

He got out his leather bag and counted out twenty sovereigns. I saw he had plenty more, so I would not bet him less than one hundred sovereigns. He put them up, and I put up $500 in greenbacks. He turned the card and lost. My partner made him believe that he had made a mistake, by showing him that the corner of the baby ticket was still turned up.

My partner wanted to bet with me, so I bet him for $500 and he won.

That made Johnnie Bull hot, as he did not have any more ready money except maybe $50. I saw he was ready for anything, so I told him I would bet him $1,000 against his gun if it was on the table. He jumped up, went to his room, and soon returned with his case. He unlocked it and showed me his gun. I put $1,000 in the barkeeper's hands, as I wanted to get the gun where he could not snatch it and run, as I expected he would do, if I gave him a chance. I mixed the cards, and he went for the baby, but he must have been excited, for he missed it. It was fun to see him. He looked at the cards, at me and my partner, then at his gun case, but it was behind the bar, and he could not get it. As soon as he could speak he said: "Oh! my gun; I've lost my gun."

He walked up and down the guards, coming in every moment to look at his gun. I finally told him if he would raise the money I would let him have his gun for $500. Then he was happy, but he would not go to bed or leave the bar for fear I would get off with his fine English gun. The next morning he told his companions, and they raised the $500 in less than no time. I heard them talking. One would say to another: "The lad has lost his gun, lads, and we must get the bloody thing for 'im."

I could have got $1,000 for it just as quick as the $500. I tried to show the other Johnnie Bulls how the lad lost his gun, but they would not come within a mile of the table. I bid them all good-bye and left the boat at Vicksburg, but I was always sorry I did not keep that gun.

The moral is simple, as Aesop might say: Stay away from three-card monte.

BIBLIOGRAPHY

BOOKS

Birchell, Donna Blake. *Wicked Women of New Mexico.* Gloucestershire, UK: The History Press, 2014.

Burns, Walter Noble. *The Saga of Billy the Kid.* Garden City, NY: Garden City Publishing, 1925.

Convis, Charles L. *Gamblers.* St. Paul, MN: Pioneer Press, 2000.

DeArment, Robert K. *Bat Masterson: The Man and the Legend.* Norman: University of Oklahoma Press, 1989.

Gardner, Mark Lee. *To Hell on a Fast Horse.* New York: William Morrow, 2010.

James, Ronald M. *The Roar and the Silence: A History of Virginia City and the Comstock Lode.* Reno: University of Nevada Press, 1998.

James, Thomas. *Three Years Among the Indians and Mexicans.* Lincoln: University of Nebraska Press, 1984.

Lee, Katie. *Ten Thousand Goddam Cattle.* Albuquerque: University of New Mexico Press, 1973.

Maskelyne, John Nevil. *Sharps and Flats: A Complete Revelation of the Secrets of Cheating at Games of Chance and Skill.* New York: Longmans, Green, and Co., 1894).

McManus, James. *Cowboys Full: The Story of Poker.* London, UK: Picador, 2009.

Metz, Leon. *John Wesley Hardin: Dark Angel of Texas.* El Paso, TX: Mangan Books, 1996.

Riley, Glenda, and Richard W. Etulain, eds. *By Grit and Grace: Eleven Women Who Shaped the American West.* Golden, CO: Fulcrum Publishing, 1997.

Sharpe, Graham. *Poker's Strangest Hands: Extraordinary But True Stories.* London, UK: Robson Books, 2007.

Tanner, Karen Holliday. *Doc Holliday: A Family Portrait.* Norman: University of Oklahoma Press, 1998.

Twain, Mark. *Roughing It.* Mineola, NY: Dover Publications, 2003.

Utley, Robert M. *Billy the Kid: A Short and Violent Life.* Lincoln: University of Nebraska Press, 1989.

Williamson, G. R. *Frontier Gambling.* Createspace Independent Publishing Platform, United States, 2011

Woog, Adam. *Wyatt Earp (Legends of the Wild West).* Chelsea House Publishing, Broomall, PA, 2010.

Wright, Robert Marr. *Dodge City, the Cowboy Capital, and the Great South-west in the Days of the Wild Indian, the Buffalo, the Cowboy, Dance Halls, Gambling Halls and Bad Men.* Wichita, KS: Wichita Eagle Press, 1913.

PERIODICALS

Abilene Chronicle, September 14, 1871.

"Amarillo Slim," obituary, *The Economist*, May 12, 2012, https://www.economist.com/obituary/2012/05/12/amarillo-slim.

Enss, Chris. "Wicked Woman Wednesday: Belle Starr," *Cowgirl*, January 20, 2016, https://cowgirlmagazine.com/wicked-women-wednesday-belle-starr.

Foley, Stephen. "One of a Kind: Legendary Gambler Amarillo Slim Has Played His Final Hand," *Independent*, May 1, 2012, https://www.independent.co.uk/news/world/americas/one-of-a-kind-legendary-gambler-amarillo-slim-has-played-his-final-hand-7697721.html.

Jay, Roger. "The Gamblers' War in Tombstone," *Wild West*, October 2004, pp. 38–45, 73.

"Reformation in Abilene," *Overland Monthly*, March 1869.

WEBSITES

http://www.cardplayer.com/pokernews/14681menofactionrich
    ardthebigbluffernixon

http://www.garlandhistorical.org/onlineresources/offerings
    printedarticles/45individualsandfamilies/152bellestarrmade
    hermarkonarea

http://www.historicdelano.com/HistoricDelano/history.php

http://www.history.com/thisdayinhistory/johnwesleyhardin
    arrivesinabilene

http://www.historynet.com/reignoftheroughscufflawandlucrein
    wichita.htm

http://www.johnnyhughes.com/story6.html

http://www.legendsofamerica.com/ksdodgehistoricaltext6.html

http://www.legendsofamerica.com/welukeshort4.html

http://www.legendsofamerica.com/wepokeralice.html

http://www.legendsofamerica.com/wewildbill.html

http://www.legendsofamerica.com/wewyattearp.html

http://www.palacesantafe.com/dining/saloon/

https://www.pokernews.com/news/2016/08/poker-pop-culture
    -015-immoral-to-let-a-sucker-keep-his-money-25520.htm

http://www.texascooppower.com/texas_stories/history/bawdy
    bellestarr

https://truewestmagazine.com/ashortstorm/

https://www.visitwichita.com/blog/post/chisholmtrail150th
    anniversaryinwichita

Index

About the Author

Ralph Estes is the author of numerous scholarly books and articles as well as the popular work of fiction, *My Own Story: The Autobiography of Billy the Kid*. Professor emeritus at the American University, Washington, DC, he now lives in New Mexico, where he is a New Mexico State Chautauqua troubadour, performing *Me and Billy*, a one-man show about the outlaw Billy the Kid, across the state.